WHAT ARE THEY SAYING ABOUT
THE HISTORICAL JESUS?

What Are They Saying About the Historical Jesus?

David B. Gowler

PAULIST PRESS
New York/Mahwah, NJ

Cover design by James Brisson
Book design by Theresa M. Sparacio

Library of Congress Cataloging-in-Publication Data

Gowler, David B., 1958–
    What are they saying about the historical Jesus? / David B. Gowler.
      p. cm.—(What are they saying about—)
    Includes bibliographical references.
    ISBN 978-0-8091-4445-7 (alk. paper)
    1. Jesus Christ—Historicity. I. Title.
BT303.2.G69 2007
232—dc22

                         2006034279

Published by Paulist Press
997 Macarthur Boulevard
Mahwah, New Jersey 07430

www.paulistpress.com

Printed and bound in the
United States of America

Contents

For
Camden D. Gowler
and
Jacob D. Gowler

May Jesus' message of justice, love, and peace
be a driving force in your lives

Preface

> I often ask myself why Jesus counts so little among great
> theologians. Certainly the difficulty of establishing his role,
> of establishing a historically presentable picture of him, has
> something to do with it. But could it not be that there has
> always been a suspicion that once one admits the historical
> Jesus one admits a proclamation aimed at changes not only
> in the church but also throughout society?[1]

The continually increasing and, to some, bewildering array
of recent studies on the historical Jesus reflects the diversity
among scholars—and people at large—about current perceptions
of "who Jesus was." The evidence is complicated because the
canonical gospels present somewhat divergent portraits of Jesus,
and extracanonical sources present an even more complex situation. In addition, our presuppositions and biases—seen and
unseen, admitted and denied—enter the mix. We always,
inevitably and understandably, project a bit of ourselves and of
our own epoch onto our conception of Jesus.

Since the torrent of books about the historical Jesus has
begun to subside (for the time being), now is a good time to
reevaluate what has been gained—and perhaps lost—in historical
Jesus scholarship over the past few years.

It also is a good time to question a few common (mis)con-
ceptions in current scholarship. Some recent commentators, for
example, stress that certain portraits of Jesus are "more Jewish"

than others and therefore more credible. The real question is not *whether* Jesus' teaching was "Jewish" but what *type* of Jewish teaching it was.[2] Some scholars are either unwilling or unable to see the full range of the dialogues in the gospels with various cultural traditions.

This book also will address, in part, the academic amnesia I have observed in recent meetings with colleagues in the *Studiorum Novi Testamenti Societas* and the Society of Biblical Literature. It is reminiscent of the problem about which Albert Schweitzer observed, "No one can justly criticize, or appraise the value of, new contributions to the study of this subject unless [that person] knows in what forms they have been presented before."[3] Indeed, many of the comments of my colleagues about the historical Jesus at recent academic conferences would have, in Schweitzer's words, "ceased to walk" if the scholars who regard a book such as David Friedrich Strauss's *The Life of Jesus Critically Examined* as obsolete "would only take the trouble to read it" (xiii). With all of the faults in Strauss's work, much current scholarship is either ignoring or blissfully unaware of the critical issues he and others raised concerning the gospel texts.

In society at large, the continuing "domestication" of Jesus—the taming of Jesus' message that glosses over his radical critique of society—is even more distressing. Jesus' teachings are often distorted beyond recognition and even hijacked to promote agendas that I believe Jesus would find abhorrent. Jesus was a prophet of an oppressed people; part of his mission was "to comfort the afflicted and to afflict the comfortable."[4] If we listen to the voice of Jesus, we can still hear the prophetic message of this first-century peasant artisan who proclaimed not only a message of hope for the oppressed but also one of judgment upon an exploitative, dominant class. That prophetic voice should haunt Christians like me who live in a nation that dominates the world politically, economically, and militarily. As Thomas Merton observed:

> If the "Gospel is preached to the poor," if the Christian mes-
> sage is essentially a message of hope and redemption for the
> poor, the oppressed, the underprivileged and those who
> have no power humanly speaking, how are we to reconcile
> ourselves to the fact that Christians belong for the most part
> to the rich and powerful nations of the earth?[5]

This book therefore is not just an academic exercise. It incorporates aspects of my own academic and spiritual journey. Over 27 years ago, I was a chemical engineering student at the University of Illinois. During my junior year, however, I began my own quest for the historical Jesus. After taking some philosophy courses and religion courses, I made two decisions: to become a religion major and to try to become a college professor. Needless to say, I did not "find" the historical Jesus during that initial semester of study; instead I discovered that I wanted to devote my life to the study of the New Testament and in doing so continue my own quest for the historical Jesus.

When Lawrence Boadt, the president of Paulist Press, and I first talked about this book, he suggested that, because of the immense amount of material in historical Jesus studies, I should focus in detail on a very limited number of scholars. So this book highlights only a small number of important works on the historical Jesus. Needless to say, maintaining brevity was difficult. The first draft of this book was more than twice its current length, so many scholars' works I wished to include had to be omitted from the final manuscript.

I am grateful to Vernon K. Robbins and Douglas Low, who have carefully read and critiqued the manuscript of every book I have written, and to Jeffrey Gibson and Loren Rosson, who also provided judicious critiques of the manuscript for this book. When I ignored their sage advice, it was at my peril.

I am especially indebted to Gene Rackley, who established the Career Development Award at Oxford College of Emory University. The inspiring story of his own experience at Oxford College is paradigmatic of the dedication of Oxford's students, staff, and faculty and is indicative of the way that Oxford transforms the lives of its students. I received the Oxford Career Development Award in 2005, which gave me release time to finish this book, and, even more importantly, enabled me to travel to Israel to see the land in which Jesus lived and worked. I write these words, in fact, at a kibbutz in Galilee, just after having visited Nazareth and Capernaum.

I also wish to honor the person and work of my colleague, Professor Hoyt Oliver. As I finish writing this book, he is concluding a much more significant journey—forty years of teaching, challenging, and mentoring students at Oxford College of Emory University. My six years as his colleague were both a joy and an honor, and I wish him well as he continues his career as a talented *Holzschnitzer*.

Finally, to my family, I owe you a debt I can never repay. My wife Rita has been a full partner in all that we have accomplished and in all that we have been through. To our sons Camden and Jacob: You are a delight, a joy, and a gift from God. No father has been as fortunate as I. You bring joy, laughter, and love into our lives. I continue to learn from you, and I am grateful beyond measure for the blessings you bring to your mother and me. My hope is that you will continue your own quests for the historical Jesus, and that his message of justice, love, and peace will be a driving force in your lives. I dedicate this book to you, with love.

1
The Modern Quest for the Historical Jesus

"If only [Jesus] would come," whispered the child.

Hannah wrapped her daughter in a blanket and put her on her lap. "I can't go and get him. Believe me, I just can't. But I can tell you a story about him. Would you like that?"

Miriam nodded, and Hannah began....

And then she told of blind people who saw again, of lepers who were healed, of lame men who could walk again.... Miriam lapped them all up. They were her stories. She was blind and could see again. She was lame and could walk again. She was sick and got better. And she drew hope from every word.

I too listened spellbound....I noted that these poor people pinned all their hopes on such stories. In them I heard their rebellion against suffering and death. I felt that as long as these stories were told, people would not be content for men and women to hunger and thirst, be crippled and paralysed, be sick and helpless. As long as they had these stories they would have hope.[1]

People have been searching for Jesus of Nazareth since he began his public activity of teaching and healing in Galilee. The Gospel of John portrays two disciples of John the Baptist questing

1

for Jesus, for example, when they ask him, "Where are you staying?" The Johannine Jesus invites them to "come and see" (John 1:38–39a). This dramatic episode portrays how it goes for many of us: Jesus, as we encounter him in the gospels, still issues such invitations, and in response, people still seek after the elusive but compelling Jesus of Nazareth.

The modern scholarly quest for Jesus, however, is significantly different. Instead of focusing on the question, "Who is Jesus?" (the living, risen Lord whom Christians experience and worship), it primarily investigates the question, "Who was Jesus?" (the first-century Jew from Nazareth). Those two questions reflect the nuances noted by Martin Kähler about the *"sogenannte historische Jesus"* (the Jesus of [mere] history) and the *"geschichtliche biblische Christus"* (the historic "real Christ" of the Bible and Christian belief).[2] Kähler argued that Christian faith cannot be dependent on the "Jesus" (re)created by historians. The "real Jesus" is the biblical Christ.[3]

Marcus Borg differentiates between the "pre-Easter Jesus" (the historical Jesus) and the "post-Easter Jesus" (the risen Jesus of Christian experience).[4] John Dominic Crossan also speaks of the "dialectic of Jesus-then as Jesus-now" but goes on to conclude: "...Jesus may be experienced as risen Jesus through divergent modes, through justice and peace, prayer and liturgy, meditation and mysticism, but it must always be *that* Jesus and no other. There is, in other words, ever and always only one Jesus."[5]

There are also, of course, both continuity and discontinuity between the pre-Easter Jesus and the post-Easter Jesus. After Easter, however, many of Jesus' followers began to focus on the implications of his death and resurrection. The Apostle Paul, for example, proclaimed "Christ crucified and risen" but wrote very little about Jesus' life and teachings. As James D. G. Dunn notes, there are some indications that Paul "must have known and cared about the ministry of Jesus," but it was "Christ's *death* that gave the proclamation of Christ its character as 'gospel.'"[6]

Church creeds share this focus by omitting the details of Jesus' life and skipping from the virgin birth to Jesus' death and resurrection. The Apostles' Creed, for example, confesses belief in

> Jesus Christ, God's only Son, our Lord, who was conceived by the Holy Spirit, born of the Virgin Mary, suffered under Pontius Pilate, was crucified, died, and was buried; he descended to the dead. On the third day he rose again; he ascended into heaven, he is seated at the right hand of the Father, and he will come again to judge the living and the dead.[7]

As the focus shifted from the message *of* Jesus to the message *about* Jesus, the *proclaimer* of the kingdom of God became the *proclaimed* Son of God who came to suffer, die, and rise again. During this "pre-quest" period, there was no dichotomy between the pre-Easter and the post-Easter Jesus, and the four gospels, by and large, were seen as reliable, historical accounts of the life, ministry, and teaching of Jesus.[8]

The quest for the historical Jesus began during the Enlightenment, which celebrated the powers of human reason and explored the world through a scientific approach. John Locke, for example, argued that reason teaches us to understand the law that governs nature and unfolds the pattern of belief that a thoughtful person can derive from it. Locke's successors went even further; the role of reason was magnified, and the Bible was subjected to a new intense and often unsympathetic scrutiny.[9] In addition, the emphasis on reason and natural laws made some people question belief in a God who intervened in history in "supernatural" ways. David Hume, for example, declared that miracles were "the most improbable of events" and had to be explained in other ways.[10] "Scientific" investigation became the basis for evaluating the "historicity" of the gospel texts.

The Quest Begins: Reimarus[11]

Most analyses of the quest for the historical Jesus begin with Hermann Samuel Reimarus (1694–1768), an ardent champion of the "religion of reason." Although Albert Schweitzer declared that Reimarus "had no predecessors,"[12] more recent research clearly indicates that Reimarus's views were anticipated by Spinoza and Pierre Bayle, and his views on Jesus in particular were indebted to English Deists, such as Lord Edward Herbert, Thomas Woolston, and Matthew Tindal, and the Irish Deist/ Pantheist John Toland.[13]

Reimarus was reticent to publicize his work in this "age of enlightenment," because people had been ostracized, lost their jobs, imprisoned, and even executed because of their religious views.[14] Reimarus circulated an anonymous manuscript of over four thousand pages among some of his friends. From 1774 to 1778, seven fragments of this manuscript were published posthumously and anonymously by one of those friends, Gerhard Lessing.[15]

According to Reimarus, Jesus' message differed significantly from the one his followers circulated after his death (64): Jesus, who envisioned himself the Messiah, proclaimed the imminent coming of the kingdom of God on earth that would liberate the Jews from Roman oppression. Instead, he was crucified by a Roman governor. After his death, however, Jesus' followers did not want to return to the drudgery of their former lives. They most likely stole Jesus' body from the tomb (161, 164, 212), fabricated stories about his resurrection (172, 199), and invented the message of his atoning death and return in glory. They created this story "because their first hopes had failed" (151; see also 211–12).

Reimarus's historical reconstructions, such as his insistence on the apostles' deliberate deception, have been overwhelmingly rejected by scholars. The work's primary significance is that it raised key issues, such as irreconcilable differences between some gospel texts (e.g., in the resurrection narratives, 153–200).

Reimarus's distinction between the historical Jesus and the (fraudulent) recasting of his message by the apostles also assumed that it was both methodologically possible and theologically necessary to discover the historical Jesus and his message: Not only *could* the historical Jesus be recovered but he *ought* to be recovered.[16]

The Quest Continues: Strauss

David Friedrich Strauss's *Life of Jesus,* published in 1835/36 when the author was only twenty-seven, represents a "turning point in the history of the Christian faith."[17] It also represented an unexpected turning point in Strauss' life. An assistant lecturer in the theological college of the University of Tübingen, he expected to receive an appointment as a professor. Strauss had envisioned that "serious and enlightened" people would welcome the book as a liberation from dogmatism and a basis for revitalizing the "true essence" of Christian faith. Instead, it was greeted with a veritable firestorm; Strauss was both denied a professorship and relieved of his position as lecturer. Socially ostracized and deprived of his desired vocation, Strauss turned into a bitter antagonist of Christianity.[18]

Strauss rejected the traditional view that the gospels present an accurate, historical picture of Jesus. He also disagreed with Reimarus and other "rationalists" who rejected the miraculous elements in the gospels. Strauss offered a "third way," in contrast to these "traditionalist" and "rationalist" interpretations of the gospels, by labeling the miracle stories as *myths*—symbolic narratives that speak religious truths about Jesus. These religious truths are most evident whenever "known and universal laws which govern the course of events" are contravened, whenever traditions contradict each other, are internally inconsistent, or other such historical difficulties arise. These problems exist not because of a deliberate deception (*pace* Reimarus) but by a process of mythical imagination (86–92).

Strauss's critique devastated the traditionalists' belief that the gospels were literal history. His intricate analyses of such stories as the three versions of the healing of the blind man/men while Jesus is entering/leaving Jericho (Matt 20:29–34; Mark 10:46–52; Luke 18:35–43; 441–45) and the resurrection accounts in the four gospels (705–44) demonstrated that their numerous discrepancies could not be papered over.

Strauss also strongly critiqued the rationalists' view that the miracles of Jesus had to be explained in a naturalistic way (e.g., the "miracle" of the loaves and fishes occurred by Jesus' shaming people into sharing their hidden food). For Strauss, such attempts to preserve the historicity of these accounts by removing all miraculous elements overlooked the significance of the narrative itself and destroyed its entire point (46–50). Strauss's solution again was Christian *myth*: "the representation of an event or of an idea in a form which is historical, but, at the same time characterized by the rich pictorial and imaginative mode of thought and expression of the primitive ages" (53). Strauss extends this idea of myth to encompass the entire history of the life of Jesus, to recognize "mythic or mythical embellishments in every portion" of the gospels (65).

The myths of the gospels come primarily from two sources: (a) the various messianic expectations existing in first-century Judaism and (b) the "particular impression left by the personal character, actions, and fate of Jesus…which served to modify the Messianic idea in the minds of his followers" (86). The account of the transfiguration, for example, developed from the conception of Jesus as the New Moses. Jesus meets with his two forerunners, Moses and Elijah, fulfills the law and the prophets, and is "glorified on a mountain" in a way greater than Moses (87, 540–46). Through this myth, Jesus' messianic dignity is thus confirmed (545).

Strauss's contribution is difficult to overestimate. The irreconcilable differences between the gospels meant that scholars could no longer view them as unvarnished historical narratives. Strauss recognized that each text should be minutely examined before attempting to determine the historicity of the event it narrates. Strauss's powerful critique also forced discussions of the miracle stories to the sidelines for many years to come.[19]

Yet, as Albert Schweitzer would illustrate, in their efforts to disentangle Jesus of Nazareth from the Christ of the church, Reimarus, Strauss, and others who followed them did not construct "objective" portraits of Jesus; although significantly different, their portraits of Jesus were just as ideological as the one(s) constructed by the church.[20] But others, such as Ernest Renan, began to grapple with the implications of the questions they raised.

The Liberal Quest for Jesus: Renan

Ernest Renan's *The Life of Jesus* was hailed as the first *biography* of Jesus.[21] In just five months it went through eleven editions, sold an unprecedented sixty thousand copies, and was translated into German, Italian, and Dutch (with a forthcoming English translation).[22]

Renan portrayed Jesus the human being, as his chapter on the infancy and youth of Jesus demonstrates: "Jesus was born at Nazareth" (81). "He proceeded from the ranks of the people [i.e., not of the lineage of David]. His father, Joseph, and his mother, Mary, were people in humble circumstances, artisans living by their labor" (83). With these three sentences, Renan rejected the birth of Jesus in Bethlehem, his Davidic lineage, and two of the pillars of Christian orthodoxy: the virgin birth and the incarnation.[23] Because of this book, Renan was dismissed from his professorship at the Collège de France and was excommunicated from the church.[24]

Renan's book was extremely popular, however, and its novelistic approach imbued it with an aesthetic power that seemingly made first-century Palestine come alive.[25] His colorful portrait of Jesus was also supplemented by his first-hand experience of the area; he wrote the book while living in southern Lebanon. Note, for example, Renan's description of Jesus and his disciples:

> The faithful band led thus a joyous and wandering life, gathering the inspirations of the master in their first bloom. An innocent doubt was sometimes raised, a question slightly skeptical; but Jesus, with a smile or a look, silenced the objection. At each step—in the passing cloud, the germinating seed, the ripening corn—they saw the sign of the Kingdom drawing nigh; they believed themselves on the eve of seeing God, of being masters of the world; tears were turned into joy; it was the advent upon earth of universal consolation (185).

Yet appearances can be deceiving. The artistic quality of the prose is not matched by historical accuracy; the book in many ways is, as Wright notes, a "work of romantic fantasy."[26] In addition, the book also unfortunately reflects the anti-Semitism of much scholarship during this time period, which results in a false caricature of first-century Judaism.[27]

Literary Relationships among the Gospels

Strauss had demonstrated that the gospels were not equally reliable historically, so scholars began to explore more fully the dates of composition, sources of, and literary relationships among the gospels.[28] The usual assumption was—since the Gospel of John was not as reliable historically as the synoptic gospels of Matthew, Mark, and Luke—that once the problems of Matthew, Mark, and Luke's interdependence and the order of their composition were solved, the "problem" of Jesus would in large part be solved. The earliest sources would offer, it was thought, the most reliable historical data to reconstruct the historical Jesus.[29] But what was the earliest source?

For centuries, people assumed that the gospels' canonical order (i.e., Matthew, Mark, Luke, John) reflected their order of composition. Karl Lachmann, however, argued for the priority of Mark and suggested that Matthew utilized a (nonextant) separate collection of Jesus' sayings.[30] A few years later, Heinrich Julius Holtzmann also championed Markan priority and said that both Matthew and Luke used a "sayings collection" *(Spruchsammlung)*.[31]

This "four source" theory envisions Mark as the earliest gospel. Matthew was written using Mark as a source, an independent "sayings" collection called Q (short for *Quelle*, German for "source"), and a complex of other traditions labeled "M" of special material found only in Matthew. Similarly but independently of Matthew, Luke used Mark and Q as sources, as well as other traditions ("L") of material found only in Luke.

Gospel Relationships and the Liberal Quest for Jesus

Foundational to the Liberal Quest was the belief that one could establish through historical-critical methodology the authentic teaching and historical person of Jesus. The "historical core" of the gospel narratives would illumine *"wie es eigentlich gewesen ist"* (what actually happened). This reconstructed historical Jesus was the legitimate object of faith—not the traditional Jesus proclaimed by the church—and his teaching should be learned and imitated.[32]

The Gospel of Mark, which many now saw as the oldest and essentially most historical gospel, became more important for interpreting Jesus' life and thought. Jesus' inner development also became important, because of the influence of the Romantic movement—which stressed the essential goodness of human beings, valued emotion and imagination over reason, and believed that feeling afforded "an immediate experience of reality."[33] Thus the Liberal lives of Jesus included discussions about Jesus' religious feelings and the development of his "messianic consciousness."

Liberal Protestant theologians in the quest for Jesus, such as Albrecht Ritschl and Adolf von Harnack, sought to free the historical Jesus from the dogma of the church. Both Ritschl and Harnack focused on how Jesus' moral teachings could be applied to life in the contemporary world. Ritschl, for example, argued that "true Christianity" was the spiritual and ethical religion based on Jesus as redeemer and founder of the kingdom of God. People, as the children of God, were to live moral lives devoted to the ethic of love.[34]

Harnack's six lectures at the University of Berlin, however, were perhaps the most famous of the Liberal statements about Christianity.[35] Harnack emphasized that Christianity is a way of life, not a system of beliefs, dogma, or doctrine. Jesus proclaimed God as Father,[36] the brotherhood and sisterhood of human beings, the infinite value of the human soul, and the "love commandment": to love God, ourselves, and other human beings, including our enemies (51). In other words, an authentic faith in Jesus does not consist in creedal orthodoxy but of doing what Jesus did.[37]

Liberalism's message reflects in some ways the authentic voice of Jesus, such as the good news for the poor (Luke 4:16–21; 5:20). Yet, as Dunn notes, the stress on individuals and not institutions/groups was a serious flaw that made Liberalism less effective.[38] In addition, Liberalism's "Jesus" was greatly removed from Jesus' actual first-century social and historical contexts; Liberalism instead created a Jesus in its own image. Such subjectivity should not be surprising, because, as Albert Schweitzer observed, authors in every epoch create a historical Jesus that is in part a reflection of themselves and their era: "each individual created [Jesus] in accordance with his own character. There is no historical task which so reveals a man's true self as the writing of a Life of Jesus."[39]

Initial Cracks in the Foundation of the Liberal Quest: Mark's Messianic Secret

Many of the nineteenth-century Lives of Jesus assumed that Mark's narrative was essentially historical. William Wrede, however, took direct aim at this misconception in his 1901 book, *The Messianic Secret:* "It must be frankly said that Mark no longer has a real view of the historical life of Jesus."[40]

Scholars who relied on Mark's historicity had made a critical mistake: Wrede demonstrated that certain motifs in Mark were not easily explained as simple, historical observations, such as Mark's theme of Jesus keeping his Messiahship a secret.[41] This "Messianic Secret" was actually a theological construction that stemmed primarily from Mark. Thus Mark's Gospel could not be used to reconstruct the development of Jesus' messianic consciousness, because Mark reflects the developing Christology of the early church. After Wrede, it would no longer be possible — try as some might — for scholars to regard the gospels as "objective" reports of the life and teachings of Jesus. In fact, scholars could no longer take it for granted that traditions in the gospels attributed to Jesus are authentically from Jesus, because the gospels are the result of a complex process of oral tradition and written composition. Wrede's work thus heightened skepticism about the likelihood of success and theological value of a historical reconstruction of the life of Jesus.[42]

The Collapse of the Liberal Quest: The Apocalyptic Prophet/Messiah[43]

The Jesus constructed by Liberalism was shattered around the turn of the century by the (re)emergence of eschatology (belief about events occurring at the end of time).[44]

Johannes Weiss

Johannes Weiss argued that a study of Jewish apocalyptic literature demonstrated that Jesus' message of the kingdom was apocalyptic—the end of the world was imminent—and could not be equated with ethical conduct or the Christian community envisioned by Liberalism.[45]

For Weiss, Jesus' concept of the kingdom of God is that it breaks out of an "overpowering divine storm" (129) as an imminent other-worldly event brought about by God alone (133). The kingdom is radically future, in no way present, and will bring the present age to an end. Jesus thus did not inaugurate the kingdom, but he waited for God to establish it in the near future (78).

Albert Schweitzer

The most notable proponent of this "apocalyptic Jesus" was Albert Schweitzer—famed biblical scholar, brilliant organist, and winner of the 1952 Nobel Peace Prize for his work as a medical missionary in West Africa. Schweitzer's *The Quest of the Historical Jesus* summarized and critiqued the disparate Lives of Jesus that had been written to that point. Yet Schweitzer pushed the apocalyptic envelope further: Weiss emphasized the centrality of eschatology in Jesus' proclamation of the kingdom; Schweitzer believed that this imminent eschatology determined "the whole course of Jesus' life" (212).

According to Schweitzer, Jesus' belief that he was the Messiah was a significant "factor in his public ministry."[46] Schweitzer even argued, unlike his contemporary Wrede, that the disciples were not aware of Jesus' identity as the Messiah until Jesus revealed it to them at Caesarea Philippi.[47]

Schweitzer's Jesus was obsessed with the apocalyptic expectation that the kingdom of God would, in the very first year of his ministry, erupt into human history to bring the world to an end. At the transfiguration, for example, "Jesus and his immediate followers were at that time in an enthusiastic state of intense eschatological expectation" (345). Jesus also was deluded into thinking that God designated him to be the Messiah, the agent who brought about that end.[48] Matthew 10:23, in which Jesus sends the Twelve on a missionary journey, provides a crucial point in this scenario: "...you will not have gone through all the towns of Israel before the Son of Man comes." Schweitzer concluded that Jesus did not expect to see them return, because the parousia of the Son of man "will take place before they have completed a hasty journey through the cities of Israel to announce it" (327).

Jesus, then, was mistaken; he awaited the parousia "in vain" (331), and this delay caused an alteration in his expectations (328). At Caesarea Philippi, Jesus' own suffering and death in Jerusalem became the primary focus and the catalyst for the inbreaking of the kingdom: "He must suffer for others...that the Kingdom may come" (347).[49] Because the kingdom did not arrive during the sending of the Twelve, Jesus reflected on the Suffering Servant in Isaiah 53 and became (erroneously) convinced that God was willing to spare others from such suffering if Jesus himself suffered and died.[50]

Jesus was mistaken again; he died, and the kingdom did not come. In one of the most famous and incessantly quoted sections of *Quest*—one which scholars seldom note that Schweitzer omitted from his 1913 revision—Schweitzer writes:

> Jesus...in the knowledge that he is the coming Son of Man lays hold of the wheel of the world to set it moving on that last revolution which is to bring all ordinary history to a close. It refuses to turn, and He throws Himself on it. Then it does turn; and crushes Him. Instead of bringing in the eschatological conditions, He has destroyed them. The wheel rolls onward, and the mangled body of the one immeasurably great Man, who was strong enough to think of Himself as the spiritual ruler of mankind and to bend his-

tory to His purpose, is hanging upon it still. That is His victory and His reign (1968: 370–71).

Schweitzer's work is significant for a number of reasons, including warnings about:

The Peril of Modernizing Jesus. As Schweitzer aptly notes, "[T]he historical Jesus will be to our time a stranger and an enigma....He passed by our time and returned to his own" (478). The problem, for Schweitzer, not only dwells in the difficulties of reconstructing a historical Jesus but also exists in the fundamental question of how a deluded first-century apocalypticist could be relevant for modern people.

The Peril of Domesticating Jesus. People often "domesticate" Jesus by ignoring his radical message and social critique. As Schweitzer writes, "[N]otice what they have made of the great imperious sayings of the Lord, how they have watered down his imperative world-denying demands on individuals.... Some of the greatest sayings are found lying in a corner like explosive shells from which the charges have been removed" (480). Jesus was a prophet of an oppressed people, and part of hearing his voice is rediscovering the first-century peasant artisan who proclaimed not only a message of hope for the oppressed but also an eschatological message of judgment upon the wealthy who exploited them.

*The Peril of **Not** Modernizing Jesus.* The great historical, social, and cultural divides between us and first-century Mediterranean peoples are even greater than Schweitzer imagined. The challenge therefore is to modernize Jesus and his message *authentically* to make them more relevant, not to domesticate Jesus or anachronize his radical message.

The Difficulty of a Relevant Historical Jesus. How can a deluded and mistaken apocalypticist be relevant for twenty-first-century people? Schweitzer argued that it occurs through mystical experience: "Jesus means something to our world because a mighty spiritual force streams forth from him and flows through our time also" (479).[51] The resulting spirit of Christ sent out into the world frees (and should impel) Christians to follow Jesus' "religion of love" in their own lives.

Most historical Jesus studies that appeared in the years after Schweitzer's book were relatively chastened by his critique. More recent studies are sometimes less chastened, but interpreters still struggle with the issues he raised, especially whether Jesus was an apocalyptic prophet who preached the imminent end of the world. The answer to that question may be, in fact, the single most important historical answer about Jesus, because it is tied directly to the essential nature of his person, message, and mission.[52]

The Partial Eclipse of the Historical Jesus[53]

After Schweitzer, many scholars believed that it was methodologically impossible to "recover" the historical Jesus and theologically unnecessary to base one's faith on the uncertain results of historical research.

Rudolf Bultmann, for example, argued that the historical Jesus was irrelevant for Christian faith and life. Bultmann tried to communicate the Christian message to twentieth-century persons, so he "demythologized" the language of the New Testament by interpreting it as a concern for "authentic" existence. Bultmann was indebted to the existentialist philosophy of Martin Heidegger, but whereas Heidegger saw authentic existence as a resolute decision to live life more authentically in light of the inescapable reality of death, Bultmann envisioned authentic existence as a response of faith to an encounter with the Word of God. This faith, however, is not in the historical Jesus; it is an individual's positive response to the church's *kerygma* (proclamation) of Jesus as the Christ.[54]

Bultmann distinguished the historical Jesus (the "Proclaimer") from the historic Christ (the "Proclaimed"), who is the true object of Christian faith, because faith is independent of tendentious historical research. In addition, the gospels are products of the preaching of early Christians and cannot be used as reliable sources for a "Life of Jesus." All we can or need to know about the historical Jesus is his understanding of existence that can be gleaned from his teachings. The self-consciousness of Jesus, however, is not a legitimate undertaking, because "...we can know almost nothing concerning the life and personality of Jesus...."[55] Yet Bultmann goes on to say, "Little as we know of [Jesus'] life and personality, we know enough of his *message* to make for ourselves a consistent picture" (12).

Since Bultmann believed that the traditions about Jesus in the gospels reflected a series of layers, he undertook the sometimes "difficult and doubtful" task of attempting to separate those layers:

> We can only count on possessing a genuine similitude of Jesus where, on the one hand, expression is given to the contrast between Jewish morality and piety and the distinctive eschatological temper which characterized the preaching of Jesus; and where on the other hand we find no specifically Christian features.[56]

This quote captures the essence of one of the most important criteria in post-Bultmannian studies of the historical Jesus, what Norman Perrin called the *criterion of dissimilarity:* For a saying of Jesus to be considered "authentic," it must be different in content from conceptions current in Judaism before Jesus or in the early Christian communities after Jesus.[57]

Bultmann thus seeks to examine elements derived from the Aramaic traditions of "the oldest Palestinian community," although even those traditions are not necessarily from Jesus (13). He peels the layers of tradition back to a core of approximately twenty-five sayings, or about forty-one verses; from this small amount of tradition, Bultmann builds an "impressive sketch of the teaching of Jesus."[58]

Bultmann concludes that Jesus did not claim to be the Messiah (9, 26). Jesus took for granted, as did his contemporaries, that the kingdom of God was to come (soon) for the benefit of the Jewish people (30, 43). Yet, in Bultmann's existential "demythologizing," the coming of the kingdom of God's real significance is that human beings are standing in a crisis of decision before God (51–52).

Conclusion

Stratifying historical Jesus scholarship into chronological categories is heuristically helpful but sometimes misleading.[59] Bultmann's era, for example, is often labeled the "no quest period," although it actually was only a "partial eclipse." In many quarters, especially in British and American scholarship, the quest for Jesus continued unabated, in an "endless procession of Lives of Jesus."[60] Yet by the 1950's, Bultmann's skepticism had influenced many scholars to abandon the quest.[61]

By shifting attention from the historical Jesus to "the Word," Bultmann hoped to avoid many of the pitfalls that plagued the various Lives of Jesus. Yet Bultmann was enmeshed in the same trap, because he *re*mythologized the teachings of an ancient Jewish apocalypticist to make them relevant for the twentieth century: Jesus calls us "to *decision*—decision between good and evil, decision for God's will or for [our] own will" (83–84). The *message* of Jesus offered by Bultmann challenged twentieth-century persons who lived through the great wars of that era, but the pitfalls outlined by Schweitzer still remained. Bultmann's Jesus was to a large extent a reflection of Bultmann, and the partial eclipse of the historical Jesus lasted until Bultmann's own students proposed a way in which the study of Jesus could once again emerge from his shadow.

2
The Continuing Quest for the Historical Jesus

> [I]t cannot be seriously maintained that the Gospels and their tradition do not allow enquiry after the historical Jesus. Not only do they allow, they demand this effort.[1]

Rudolf Bultmann's skepticism about the quest for the historical Jesus cast a long shadow, but ironically, it was Bultmann's former students who inaugurated a "New Quest" for Jesus.

Ernst Käsemann

On October 20, 1953, in Jugenheim, Germany, Ernst Käsemann's lecture to a reunion of Bultmann's former Marburg students inaugurated the New Quest for the historical Jesus. Käsemann's lecture was eventful not only because of what he said, but because a former student of Bultmann said it. In contrast to Bultmann, Käsemann thought that it was methodologically possible to reach (limited) historical conclusions about Jesus of Nazareth and theologically necessary to do so, because there is some continuity between the historical human being Jesus and the Christ of faith.[2]

Käsemann noted that any attempt to free the historical Jesus from the "fetters" of church dogma was destined to fail, because we only learn about him through the early church's *kerygma* and dogma (17). Käsemann called for a *via media:* The historical elements in the synoptics cannot be altogether rejected, because history is accessible only through tradition and comprehensible only through interpretation (18). Ironically, this creates a paradox: The early Christian community wanted to maintain historical continuity with Jesus but had to replace him with its own message to do so. "Mere history" becomes "significant history" through such interpretation (20–21).

As a result, the historical Jesus meets us in the New Testament, but *not* "as he was," but as "Lord of the community which believes in him."[3] Thus any "Life of Jesus" which attempts to delineate the actual course of his life or inner development is for the most part "groping in darkness" (23). Yet we cannot "choke off the question" about the Jesus of history, because interest in Jesus himself generated and formed the gospels. Although the gospel authors did not arrive at a "monochrome outlook," they agreed on one thing: "the life history of Jesus was constitutive for faith, because the earthly and the exalted Lord are identical." Therefore, Käsemann argued, the quest for the historical Jesus is a theological necessity; otherwise, the *kerygma* of the church becomes docetic mythology (33–34).

Since we cannot assume the historical reliability of the synoptic traditions,[4] Käsemann suggested formal criteria to identify the authentic teachings of Jesus (35). The criterion of dissimilarity, for example, provides "more or less safe ground under our feet" (37) and, if one proceeds carefully, "certain characteristic traits in his preaching stand out in relatively sharp relief" (46).

Käsemann uses this criterion to find the distinctive element in the mission of Jesus (37–45): The first and fourth antitheses of the Sermon on the Mount, for example, presuppose a person who embodies a claim above that of Moses (since Jesus rivals and challenges Moses). To this, there are no Jewish parallels, and the only category into which these statements place Jesus is that of Messiah. Other distinctive words and actions of Jesus—such as his proclamation of the kingdom of God—also place him in the role of the Messiah. Käsemann, though—in arguments dependent upon Bultmann—believed that Jesus never explicitly claimed to be the Messiah. The full implications of Jesus' words and actions were understood later by the early Christian community (43–44): Jesus "never claimed to be and yet was—their Lord" (47).

Käsemann wanted to reanimate discussions among Bultmann's former pupils and, hopefully, persuade Bultmann to rethink some of his "exaggerated" and "theologically dangerous" historical skepticism.[5] Käsemann certainly reanimated the discussions, but Bultmann reacted vehemently to this New Quest. Bultmann argued that he had never denied the continuity between Jesus and the *kerygma*. Instead, he distinguished *historical* continuity from *material (sachlich)* continuity between the Jesus of history and the *kerygma* of the early church. Of course, there is *historical* continuity, he argued, but not *material* continuity.[6] Jesus of Nazareth and the *kerygma* are historical phenomena, but the risen Christ is not, so any use of historical investigations to "legitimize" the *kerygma* is futile, misguided, and does not recognize its true nature.

Käsemann (over)responded to what he saw was an unfair attack from his former professor.[7] Although he detected some "extensive" and "very astonishing concessions" by Bultmann (50),[8] he vividly expressed his frustration at Bultmann's "extraordinarily radical antithesis" between historical and material continuity of Jesus and the primitive Christian preaching (36).

Ernst Fuchs

Despite Bultmann's reservations and the acrimonious split with Käsemann, other former students of Bultmann took up this New Quest. Three years after Käsemann's lecture, Ernst Fuchs

delivered a lecture at the University of Zurich in which he proposed that knowledge about Jesus' message could be based on the
correlation between his actions and teachings.[9] The parable of the
Prodigal Son, for example, was Jesus' defense of his eating with
tax collectors and sinners (53).

Fuchs envisioned the parables as verbalizing Jesus' personal
understanding of existence: The "immediate meaning of Jesus"
cannot be answered apart from the historical Jesus (19). But
Fuchs was *not* talking about "facts" in the sense of specific historical events in Jesus' life and ministry. Instead, parables are "language events" in which Jesus' understanding of his own
existence, situation, and faith "enters language" and is still available for us to share.

Günther Bornkamm

Six months after Fuchs's lecture, Günther Bornkamm published the only full-length book from the New Questers: *Jesus of
Nazareth*. Bornkamm noted the impossibility of writing a biography of Jesus: "No one is any longer in the position to write a life
of Jesus" (13). It is possible, however, to arrive at a reliable
understanding of Jesus' thought and teaching, to achieve a sound
picture of the type of person Jesus was, and to understand what he
was trying to accomplish (14).

Bornkamm agreed that "genuine faith" was not dependent
upon historical Jesus research (15) and that there was continuity
between Jesus of Nazareth and the Christ of faith (17). The
nature of gospel traditions demands inquiry into the historical
Jesus, because those traditions are concerned with the pre-
Easter history of Jesus (22). Despite its limitations, the primitive tradition is "brim full of history" (26). Therefore, the
sources permit Bornkamm to "compile the main historically
indisputable traits and to present the rough outlines of Jesus'
person and history" (53):

Jesus was a Jew from "semi-pagan despised Galilee." His family lived in Nazareth, his father was a carpenter, and we know the names of four of his brothers (53). Jesus spoke Aramaic, but as a Jewish rabbi must have been able to understand the Hebrew of the Bible. We do not know if Jesus spoke any Greek, but he displays "no trace of the influence of Greek philosophy or of the Greek manner of living" (54).

Jesus' baptism by John is one of the most "certainly verified occurrences of his life." Although this baptism had far-reaching importance, we cannot know what it meant for Jesus, his decisions, or his inner development (54). We can, however, learn much about his teaching, conflicts with opponents, healing activities, that he gathered disciples, that people flocked to him, and that his enemies arise and increase (54). The last decisive turning point in his life was the trip to Jerusalem with his message of the kingdom of God. He ended up on a Roman cross (55).

Jesus' message is closely allied to the apocalyptic expectations of his day. The day of judgment will soon dawn violently, although Jesus is reticent to speak of the day or hour (66–67). Jesus' core message is that God will reign; the kingdom's imminent arrival can be seen in Jesus' words and deeds—the blind see, the lepers are cleansed, the deaf hear, and the dead are raised. Jesus calls people to repent and to accept God's invitation in light of this dawning of God's reign (82–83). Although Jesus never claimed to be the Messiah, "the Messianic character of his being is contained *in* his words and deeds and *in* the unmediatedness of his historic appearance" (178).

Bornkamm's book sounded familiar albeit limited themes, and his synthesis of the teachings of Jesus was neither groundbreaking nor earth-shattering. In addition, the theologian Bornkamm was evident in his reconstructed historical Jesus. As William Herzog notes, "Bornkamm spins his version of the familiar tale of the existential Jesus whose understanding of existence becomes the basis for the *kerygma* of the early church."[10]

Hans Conzelmann

Hans Conzelmann briefly entered the fray in 1958 with an essay that was later expanded into the short book, *Jesus*.[11] Conzelmann echoed the existentialist perspectives of Käsemann, Fuchs, and Bornkamm, but he offered a distinctive element by arguing that Christology replaced chronology as the basic meaning of Jesus' message: Jesus had become the constitutive factor in eschatology (70–71). Jesus did not expect another Son of man to appear; neither did he think of his own future parousia as the Son of man. Instead Jesus offered the proclamation that what is happening *now* is the *complete, final* announcement; "only the kingdom of God itself is to follow" (77).[12]

James M. Robinson

James Robinson's friendly summary gave the New Quest its name.[13] He argued that the "objective historical method" of the original quest—which focused on mundane data such as names, places, dates, causes and effects—fell far short of uncovering the "deeper level of reality" of the historical Jesus (e.g., his understanding of existence and the continuing significance of his life and teachings; 28–29).

Robinson believed that the New Quest offered a "new concept of history and the self" (66–67). In spite of difficulties, the *kerygma* of the "primitive Church" provides a way to encounter "the meaning of history and the existential selfhood of persons" (69). Yet even more striking, however, is Robinson's claim that the "historical Jesus confronts us with existential decision, just as the *kerygma* does" (77), although Robinson—after hearing Bultmann's response to the New Questers—backed away from this position.[14]

Robinson thus falls into the same trap that had ensnared Schweitzer: He critiqued other scholars who had incorporated their own ideological and cultural points of view into their

understandings of Jesus, but he then presented a view of Jesus
that was greatly determined by his own ideology, culture, and
place in history.

Conclusion: The New Quest

The New Quest developed and flourished among Bultmannian scholars, so it possessed a homogeneity that previous (and
later) quests lacked. First, the gap between the historical Jesus
and the risen Christ was bridged through the *kerygma*. Second,
history was envisioned as "event" not a "sequence of facts." New
Questers focused primarily on the *teachings* of Jesus, since the
nature of the gospels precludes a biographical approach. Third,
the burden of proof now was to demonstrate that a tradition origi-
nated with Jesus.[15] The focus thus shifted to debates about criteria
and methods of investigation that could determine with any
degree of certainty the authentic teachings of Jesus.

The work of two prominent scholars illustrates the debates
during this period: Joachim Jeremias and Norman Perrin. Jeremias
took a more conservative path than members of the Bultmannian
school concerning the reliability of the traditions about Jesus.[16]
Perrin was a student of Jeremias, but he gained a deep appreciation
of the work of Bultmann and his students.

Joachim Jeremias

Jeremias's *The Parables of Jesus* (1947) actually helped pre-
pare the way for the New Quest, because he argued for some continuity between the historical Jesus and the risen Christ.[17] On one
hand, Jeremias declared, "We stand right before Jesus when reading his parables" (12). On the other hand, the parables underwent a
certain amount of reinterpretation. Jeremias articulated, however,
some "definite principles of transformation" that allowed him to

remove the husks of interpretation and reveal the kernels of Jesus' message. Jeremias's work was a significant achievement, but the transformation from the parables of Jesus to the parables as found in the gospels is more complicated than he envisioned.[18]

Jeremias's *New Testament Theology* offered a "largely neglected" approach to the teachings of Jesus—a close examination of language and style.[19] Jeremias attempted to uncover the Aramaic pattern, style, and vocabulary preferred by Jesus, such as the divine passive (9–14) or rhythmic shapes (20–29). To some extent, Jeremias built upon T. W. Manson's *The Teaching of Jesus*.[20] Jeremias, like Manson, was more confident of the reliability of the synoptic traditions than were scholars in the Bultmannian tradition, and he placed the burden of proof on those who argued for the inauthenticity of the sayings of Jesus (37).

Jeremias reworked Manson's notion of a "Remnant," the prophetic idea, developed further in Jewish apocalyptic writings, that the restoration of Israel would take place through a "saving remnant" of the people of Israel who would be a "light unto the Gentiles" (258–59). Jesus, as the eschatological Son of man, saw himself as the head of the remnant, the "true Israel" (269). Jeremias thus interpreted Jesus' message in light of Jewish apocalyptic literature: "the only significance of the whole of Jesus' activity is to gather the eschatological people of God" (170).[21]

Other scholars would take issue with Jeremias's rather sanguine view of the reliability of synoptic traditions and Jesus' statements about the imminence of the *eschaton* (e.g., Mark 9:1). Debate also raged concerning whether Jesus used the term Son of man, and, if he did, in which context(s) he used it.[22]

Norman Perrin

Norman Perrin's *Rediscovering the Teaching of Jesus* stands in a unique position: Perrin's two principal teachers had been T. W. Manson and Joachim Jeremias, but he later became an admirer of Bultmann and Bultmann's students. Perrin thus takes the "bold step" of attempting to integrate the insights of these two perspectives into his own synthesis. His attempt necessitated a focus on methodological issues, including adequate criteria to judge the authenticity of the traditions (11–12). Perrin's starting point was that *"the burden of proof will be upon the claim to authenticity"* (emphasis his; 39), and he enumerated some basic criteria for determining whether sayings came from the historical Jesus.

Perrin argued that all reconstructions of the teaching of Jesus must build upon the "fundamental criterion for authenticity," the *criterion of dissimilarity* (39). Perrin acknowledged some of the limitations of this criterion but argued that the "brutal fact of the matter is that we have no choice" (43). Others have raised serious objections against this criterion, however: There had to be some continuity between Judaism, Jesus, and early Christianity, and we do not know enough about the various streams of first-century Judaism and Christianity to determine exactly what is dissimilar. Some — albeit not all — scholars have even abandoned this criterion.[23]

Perrin's *criterion of coherence* states that material from the earliest strata of the tradition may be accepted as authentic if it coheres with material established as authentic by the criterion of dissimilarity (43). Thus, Perrin argues that the saying in Thomas 82 ("He that is near me is near the fire; he that is far from me is far from the Kingdom") is authentic, because it coheres to other authentic sayings (e.g., Mark 9:49; 12:34). Since Perrin based the use of this criterion on results from the criterion of dissimilarity, however, the same objections apply.

Perrin's *criterion of multiple attestation* states that material may be authentic if it is found widely in all (or most) of the "sources which can be discerned behind the synoptic gospels" (45). Perrin was restrained in his use of this "more objective" criterion, because, in his words, a saying still must not be "characteristic of an activity, interest, or emphasis of the earliest Church" (46).

Perrin believed he could "reconstruct major aspects of the teaching of Jesus beyond reasonable doubt" in three areas of the tradition: the parables, the kingdom of God sayings, and the Lord's Prayer (47). Perrin also decided that Jesus never predicted the future arrival of an apocalyptic Son of man (198). This concept, Perrin argues, was not found in ancient Judaism, and all such passages in the synoptics stem from Christian reflection on passages such as Daniel 7:13, Psalm 110:1, and Zechariah 12:10ff (164–83). Perrin's conclusions thus reflect the "apocalyptic Jesus" debate that still rages today.

The Continuing Quest for the Historical Jesus

Historical Jesus scholarship entered a new phase in 1985 with two divergent but signal events. First, E. P. Sanders published *Jesus and Judaism,* which attempted to answer the historical question of how Jesus could live totally within Judaism and yet be the origin of a movement that separated from Judaism.[24] The second signal event was the first meeting of the Jesus Seminar. Convened by Robert Funk, this group of scholars met twice a year for several years to compile a list of words and deeds attributed to Jesus and to determine which traditions actually stemmed from the historical Jesus.[25]

The conclusions of the Jesus Seminar and Sanders are substantially different, but both claimed that their primary interest was historical, not theological. As Walter Weaver notes, "…at this stage what seems more characteristic of this new movement is a lack of any special interest in the theological significance of its subject."[26]

Barnes Tatum, in his excellent book about the historical Jesus, declared that current historical Jesus scholars believe that Jesus research should be "methodologically possible and theologically neutral."[27] I would argue, however, that although many recent studies attempt—or say that they do—to bracket theological concerns from their investigations, such objectivity is, in practice, impossible. John Dominic Crossan is closer to the mark when he writes: "It is impossible to avoid the suspicion that historical Jesus research is a very safe place to do theology and call it history, to do autobiography and call it biography."[28] Although there is less explicit theology in most current works on the historical Jesus, theological and ideological positions underlie many of the debates.

Tatum described the current phase of historical Jesus research as "Post-Quest" (102). Other scholars adopted N. T. Wright's term: "Third Quest."[29] Wright argued that the term *Third Quest* should not be defined in a chronological way, but his use of the term is too restrictive. He suggested that the New Quest had been revived by the Jesus Seminar but argued that the term *Third Quest* should be restricted to a pool of twenty "particularly important" scholars (including him!) who placed Jesus within "apocalyptic Jewish eschatology." This perspective, Wright believed, was "where the leading edge of contemporary Jesus-scholarship is to be found."[30] Robert Funk, however, labeled such questers as Wright as "pretend questers," and scholars such as himself as "reNEWed questers." Funk minces no words: "Third questers are really conducting a search primarily for historical evidence to support claims made on behalf of creedal Christianity and the canonical gospels. In other words, the third quest is an apologetic ploy."[31]

Other scholars, such as Gerd Theissen and Annette Merz, use Third Quest in a more inclusive and chronological way. All current Jesus research is part of this Third Quest, and common elements emerge: (a) "sociological interest" replaces "theological interest"; (b) Jesus is situated within Judaism rather than distinct from Judaism; and (c) many scholars are open to using noncanonical sources.[32] Other distinctive elements of recent historical Jesus research include: (d) attention to questions broader than merely debates over the authenticity of individual sayings; (e) frequent critiques of New Quest methodology, including the criterion of dissimilarity; (f) placing the "Jewish Jesus" into a wider first-century context; and (g) openness by many scholars to interdisciplinary approaches.[33] Despite these similar features, current Jesus research includes a number of differing approaches which stem, Theissen and Merz argue, from it splitting into "different trends" (11).

Edgar McKnight concurs: "[A]ll the options in the history of Jesus research are once more available."[34] It is also clear that these different trends reflect the various ideological positions presupposed by each interpreter. These presuppositions influence where and how far they will go, as well as how they proceed. They also play a determining role in the questions they ask, and the answers they receive. Where and how they look influences what they will find and see.[35]

As John Dominic Crossan correctly noted, our best theories, methods, and models will always be dated and doomed not just when they are wrong but even when they are "right." Therefore, it is incorrect to speak of the "quest" for the historical Jesus; we should speak of our "reconstructions" of Jesus that "must be done over and over again in different times and different places, by different groups and different communities, and by every generation again and again and again."[36] Therefore Crossan speaks only of reconstructing the historical Jesus as best one can at any given time and place—with a clear method that is cogently communicated to encourage public discourse, to promote the dialectic of past and present, of "us" and "them" (44).

The term *dialogic*, however, is more apt than *dialectic*, and, in reality, the historical Jesus did not begin the dialogue. His "original" utterances were, in essence, rejoinders in dialogue with and incorporating aspects of the words of others who had preceded him, whether from the Hebrew Bible, traditional repertories, or his contemporaries. The followers of Jesus likewise entered into a dialogue with the words of Jesus. In a similar way, when Jesus' words were embedded into the gospels, the author's voice entered into a dialogue with those traditions; the author's voice then reverberated with the voice of Jesus and others who had responded to him.[37]

Although I have many difficulties with Crossan's portrait of Jesus, I believe that he is correct in designating the search for Jesus as a reconstruction. It is best not to speak of a quest; that closes off interpretation and suggests a final destination. Instead, we should speak of reconstruction, a reinterpretation in a new context that is always historical, personal, and dialogical. It is indeed a (re)construction, like an ideological bridge that is built during the process of interaction between voices, past and present.

3
The Jesus Seminar and Its Critics

> I confess I am more interested in what Jesus thought about
> God's domain than in what Peter the fisherman and Paul the
> tentmaker thought about Jesus of Nazareth.
>
> I am inclined to the view that Jesus caught a glimpse
> of what the world is really like when you look at it with
> God's eyes....
>
> I have a glimpse of the real Jesus stealing a peek at
> God's domain. My glimpse is informed by, but bypasses,
> the Jesus of the gospels—the Christ superimposed by the
> evangelists on their own glimpse of the real Jesus.[1]

Many years ago, I attended my first Society of Biblical Literature conference and attended the opening session of the Historical Jesus Section. To my dismay, this session degenerated into the speaker and an audience member personally insulting each other, a vivid illustration of how scholarly discussions about Jesus of Nazareth could become vitriolic (see Luke 12:51!).

In recent years, the debates have been the most bitter about the activities of one specific group: the Jesus Seminar. In this chapter, I hope to separate the wheat from the chaff—the fair critiques from the unfair, personal attacks—and offer an even-handed assessment of what the Jesus Seminar has or has not accomplished.[2]

The Jesus Seminar According to Robert W. Funk

In the initial, autobiographical section of his book *Honest to Jesus,* Robert Funk indicates that his drive to make scholarship public began while he was teaching at Vanderbilt's Divinity School. His desire for "intellectual freedom" then necessitated a move out of the seminary into the "secular" University of Montana. Unhappy there as well, Funk retired as soon as he could, and with his wife founded his own publishing house, Polebridge Press. Funk had "anguished" over the low level of religious literacy in the United States, so they also founded the Westar Institute as a "frontal assault" on this "pervasive religious illiteracy" (6).

The Westar Institute's first project was the Jesus Seminar, a response to "profound public ignorance" and to "an awakening in scholarly circles to new ways of viewing the Jesus tradition preserved in the gospels" (7). Funk invited about thirty colleagues to join him as "Fellows" in the Seminar to collect and analyze the words and deeds ascribed to Jesus in all ancient sources (up to 300 CE). In order to finish their work by 2000, the group agreed "reluctantly" to vote using the "now notorious colored beads" (8). Differing versions of what the colors signify have appeared— note the two options that appear in *The Parables of Jesus,*[3] the form found in *The Five Gospels,*[4] the two options listed in *The Acts of Jesus,*[5] and the explanations in Robert Miller's *The Jesus Seminar and Its Critics.*[6] In *Honest to Jesus,* however, Funk describes the colored beads this way (8):

- Red: Jesus said it or something very close to it
- Pink: Jesus probably said something like it, although his words have suffered in transmission
- Gray: These are not his words, but the ideas are close to his own
- Black: Jesus did not say it; the words represent the Christian community or a later point of view.

What Did the Jesus Seminar Really Say?

The best way to sketch the Seminar's procedures and conclusions is to focus on some of its major works:

The Parables of Jesus

The Seminar met twice a year and was co-chaired by Robert
Funk and John Dominic Crossan. Specific sayings were evaluated at each meeting, and essays were written and distributed in
advance to facilitate discussions. Consensus was reached by voting, not to "determine the ultimate truth" but to learn what the
majority among them thought was the truth (xiv).[7] *The Parables
of Jesus* is a "Red Letter Edition" that mirrors editions of the
Bible that have Jesus' words in red; this format displays the Seminar's "consensus on what parables Jesus actually told and how he
told them" (ix).

The Seminar decided that the noncanonical Gospel of
Thomas was independent of the canonical gospels, often exhib-
ited far less editorial activity than the canonical gospels, and
sometimes appeared "to be closer to an original version of a saying or parable" (11). Therefore, the Seminar included Thomas
with the synoptic gospels as principal sources for determining the
authentic parables of Jesus.[8]

The Seminar evaluated thirty-three parables, the "bedrock
of the tradition" (14, 20). It judged five parables to be "red"
(Leaven, Good Samaritan, Dishonest Steward, Vineyard Laborers, and the Mustard Seed); sixteen "pink"; six "gray"; and six
"black." Each parable was represented in the appropriate font
color, with brief annotations that explained the Seminar's decision about authenticity. For example, the Seminar concluded that
the parable of The Leaven was authentic (red in Matthew and
Luke; pink in Thomas), because the image of leaven was used in a
provocative way: In Passover observance, for example, leaven
was a negative symbol of corruption. In this parable, Jesus instead

uses leaven positively to represent the kingdom of God, and the parable provides a surprising reversal of expectations (29). The parable of the Tower Builder, on the other hand, is rated black, because it belongs to the "fund of common lore in both the Jewish and Hellenistic worlds of the time" (68).

The Emerging Jesus

In November 1989, Funk described the "Jesus" that was emerging from the Seminar's work.[9] They had evaluated 1,001 of the 1,388 sayings attributed to Jesus in all sources up to 313 CE; 291 of them were given red/pink designations. These 291 sayings, however, had parallels, so the number of "different" sayings deemed authentic was actually 65. Of the 134 sayings from Mark, only 17 (12.67%) garnered a red/pink vote. Of the 268 items in Q, 111 (41%) received red/pink designations. In the Gospel of Thomas, 22 percent of the sayings (25 of 114) were voted red/pink.

The Seminar reported its progress in eight major areas:

1. *Emerging Data and Trends*
   a. Jesus' precise words will never be recovered: He spoke Aramaic (the gospels are in Greek), and over two decades of oral transmission hopelessly obscured them.
   b. Jesus' characteristic speech was aphorisms, parables, and challenge-riposte exchanges; his language was pithy, vivid, and often humorous with caricature, hyperbole, or paradox.
   c. The Seminar gave more weight to traditions from what they viewed as the earliest layers of the tradition (Q or Thomas) or to those sayings found in two or more independent sources.
   d. Fellows were skeptical of any saying in which Jesus referred to himself, except as a member of the human race (e.g., the Son of man has nowhere to lay his head), or which was couched in language distinctive to the gospel authors.

e. Jesus' coherent vision was expressed in unsystematic and occasional ways.

2. *A Non-apocalyptic Jesus*. Since an astonishing 97 percent of the Fellows agreed that Jesus did not expect the world to end soon, the Seminar reported that the scholarly view of an apocalyptic Jesus had "died a scholarly death" (11).

Burton Mack's paper, "The Kingdom Sayings in Mark," presented at the Fall 1986 meeting, serves as a good example of how the Seminar reached this conclusion.[10] Mack argued that Jesus used the term *kingdom* more like a Cynic-sage than an apocalyptic prophet; the cultural frame is primarily Hellenistic wisdom, not Jewish apocalyptic. Mark creatively reinterpreted earlier nonapocalyptic materials apocalyptically, and Mack concluded that no kingdom saying in Mark is authentic. Q and the Gospel of Thomas provide better evidence for Jesus' use of the term.

This "scholarly death" of the apocalyptic Jesus, however, was greatly exaggerated, and it became one of the more controversial elements of the Seminar's "Jesus."

3. *Passion, Trial, Death*. The Seminar decided that no saying attributed to Jesus in the passion narratives was authentic. More than 97 percent of the Fellows were convinced that Jesus did not predict his own death, and a similar 97 percent believed that there was no Jewish trial nor any Jewish crowd involved in Jesus' condemnation by Pilate. Jesus was handed over to Pilate by the leading priests and executed on Pilate's authority (153).

Once again, these results reflect the Seminar's lack of trust in the reliability of the Gospel of Mark. The passion narrative stories are largely Mark's creation, reflecting the tendency of "Christian storytellers" to read back into the life of Jesus convictions they had acquired after his death.[11]

4. *Jesus' Self-assessment*. Although half of the Fellows agreed that Jesus regarded himself as anointed with the

Spirit, nearly 92 percent voted that Jesus did not believe himself to be the Messiah (12).

5. *God's Empire.* The Seminar translated *kingdom of God* as *God's empire,* and 97 percent agreed that Jesus proclaimed the presence of this empire in both deeds and words (e.g., Luke 11:20). God's empire belongs to those who least expect it, such as the poor (Luke 6:20) and not the rich (Matt 19:24), and this reversal of expectations seems to be characteristic of Jesus.

6. *Behavior in God's Empire.* The lifestyle in God's empire is conditioned by reciprocity, radical almsgiving, and other "outrageous" standards of behavior (e.g., turning the other cheek).

7. *Jesus' Behavior.* Jesus rejected the asceticism of John the Baptist, associated with the dregs of society, rejected fasting, seemed to be a homeless drifter (e.g., Luke 9:57–58), and was fond of social occasions where he ate and drank liberally (e.g., Luke 7:33–34).

8. *Conflict with Judaism.* This title was unfortunate, because the conflict actually was a conflict *within* Judaism. A majority of Fellows (62%) believed that Jesus was in conflict with Pharisees, although the gospel accounts were exaggerated. Jesus challenged Sabbath regulations, but it is unclear whether he actually broke Sabbath law. Jesus appeared to be more at odds with the Sadducees and the temple (15).

The Five Gospels: The Search for the Authentic Words of Jesus

This book reports the results of the Seminar's deliberations about more than 1,500 sayings attributed to Jesus and provides a new translation of the "five" gospels. The provocative name (the "Scholars Version") and the preface's explicit criticism of the recently published New Revised Standard Version (xiii–xv) were not well received by many scholars. The Seminar argued, however, that a translation should be in "readable English" and that the Gospel of Thomas should be included (xiii). The result is a readable but colloquial translation in "American English."[12]

In this book, the editors Robert Funk and Roy Hoover claim that the "scholarship represented by the Fellows of the Jesus Seminar is the kind that has come to prevail in all the great universities of the world" (35). In a broad sense, that may be true, but Funk's introduction to the Jesus Seminar's next book, *The Acts of Jesus,* stated: "These modest checks on the conclusions of the Fellows of the Jesus Seminar should reassure our readers that a broad consensus on both method and result does exist among critical scholars" (38).

That statement simply is untrue. There is some agreement among scholars about *method,* although less now than in previous years (e.g., the debates about the criterion of dissimilarity). As far as *result,* the veritable firestorms from many scholars that erupted against the Seminar's work amply demonstrated that no "broad consensus" existed.[13]

The Acts of Jesus: The Search for the Authentic Deeds of Jesus

The Jesus Seminar next published its assessment of "what Jesus of Nazareth did and what was done to him."[14] The data included 387 reports of 176 events. Only 10 of those events were given a red rating (reflecting a high confidence in historicity), and only 19 were colored pink (a probable event). Thus, only 16 percent of the deeds (compared to 18 percent of the sayings) were deemed accurate representations of what Jesus did and what happened to him.[15]

The Seminar used its previous assessments of the authentic sayings of Jesus as a filter through which to screen the deeds of Jesus (including the debatable assumption that only those stories in which Jesus is represented as a laconic sage are likely to be historical; 34).[16] Other criteria were added, however, such as "dramatic plausibility," the requirement that the setting, participants, and action be realistic (28).

Some of the Seminar's conclusions were not new or provocative, but others were certain to raise eyebrows if not a furor, especially among the general public. The Seminar concluded, for example, that Jesus was not born of a virgin, and his father was Joseph or some other male who either seduced or raped Mary (533). Although Jesus was seen as a healer, he only cured psychosomatic maladies and did not perform any "nature miracle." He did not claim to be the Messiah, was executed as a public nuisance, his body decayed (462), he did not rise bodily from the dead, and there was no empty tomb (533).[17]

Individual Contributions from Seminar Members

The Seminar's work expanded in several ways, most notably with many Fellows publishing their own books on the historical Jesus. These "profiles of Jesus" show widespread agreement in many areas, but they also demonstrate how members of the Seminar did not always agree with the Seminar's "consensus" views.

Honest to Jesus by Robert W. Funk

Funk proclaimed that we should "return to Nazareth," because the "true historical Jesus" should overthrow the "Christ of Christian orthodoxy and creeds" (20). Funk envisioned himself as a new Martin Luther, calling for a "powerful new reformation" (21) with his own twenty-one theses based on his "renewed" quest for Jesus (300–314). For Funk, many barriers block this return to Nazareth, such as popular images of Jesus, ignorance of the Bible, and the "foibles of biblical scholarship" (54). In many ways, Funk's book is a damning indictment of religious illiteracy and the disconnect between biblical scholarship, public discourse, and popular images of Jesus in the media.

The "authentic" parables serve as the foundation of Funk's reconstruction of Jesus. The Jesus of those parables—after Funk gets through with them—is different from Jesus the apocalyptic prophet. With these parables as the base, the aphorisms are then "tested" to determine if they have formal coherence with Jesus' parable tradition (136).

Even more fundamental to Funk's conclusions are the decisions he makes about which sources to prioritize. Funk assumes the existence of the Q source, but he also assumes the earliest traditions in Q did not contain eschatological materials and reveal a Jesus who "functioned mostly as a secular sage" (135). The "electrifying convergence" of the Gospel of Thomas and the earliest layers of the Q tradition is important, because, for Funk, Q and Thomas are independent witnesses that "antedate the Gospel of Mark by a decade or two" (137–38).[18] Funk's position was challenged by scholars who doubted the existence of Q, the ability to recover layers of tradition in Q, and/or Thomas's independence from the canonical gospels. Funk's decisions about Q and Thomas predetermine the reconstruction of his "real Jesus." If you start with these presuppositions, the end result is virtually guaranteed, as Funk himself realizes (168).

Funk's analyses often produce brilliant insights into (some of) Jesus' teachings. His discussions of what he finds to be authentic Jesus material are insightful and well written; that glass is half-full. What is missing, however, are those elements that do not survive the prism of the "earlier" Q material and its convergence with Thomas; that glass is half-empty.

For Funk, Jesus' main theme was the dominion of God, which he portrayed in terms drawn entirely from the everyday world around him (149). In Jesus' vision, the new age was beginning (166), and he challenged his listeners by reversing the platitudes of his day with unexpected twists and insights (153). Economically and socially, Jesus was a peasant, but his rhetorical skills bordered on the magical (158). He was transfixed by a vision of God's dominion that both captivated and liberated him (163). In God's dominion, reciprocity was the fundamental principle; you cannot be a recipient of forgiveness unless you become an agent of forgiveness: "It's as simple as that and as difficult as that" (213).

Funk believed that Mark created the passion narrative and that all other passion stories are based on Mark, directly or indirectly (240). Sometime after Jesus' death, his followers regrouped, formed communities, organized their memories and convictions, and became a movement (223). In the process, the sayings of Jesus were domesticated, Jesus was "marketed" as the Messiah, and the mythical Christ gradually replaced the Galilean sage (254).[19]

This book brings to mind one of the Jesus Seminar's dictums: "Beware of finding a Jesus entirely congenial to you." To be honest, I like the Jesus that Funk has reconstructed. I would love to sit around a table with that Jesus and his followers to listen, learn, and laugh. I suspect that Funk would have too. This congenial portrait of Jesus, however, inevitably leads to the question, "Did Funk create a 'real Jesus' in his own image?" Glimpses of the "real Funk" seem to indicate that he did. Funk envisioned himself as an iconoclast who did not "trust the people who are in charge" (9); his Jesus similarly shows "disdain for the priests, levites, and the temple…" (196). How much of this Galilean sage is a reflection of Funk and his own ethical horizons? Only Funk could have answered that question, but his reliance on "common sense" to eliminate data from consideration (51) or his comments about Jesus' rejection of an afterlife (215) seem to depend substantially more on Funk's worldview than that of Jesus.[20]

Jesus: A New Vision by Marcus Borg[21]

Marcus Borg, a prominent member of the Seminar and an author of numerous works on the historical Jesus, was an early proponent of a noneschatological Jesus. Borg's "temperate" position is nuanced, however, because he argues that in the "clearly authentic sayings of Jesus," the term *kingdom of God* never pointed "unmistakably" to a future temporally-conceived kingdom, although a few "may allude to that."[22] Borg's case is also grounded in his belief that the future Son of man references are not authentic. Without these sayings, Borg claims, "there is no reason to think of the kingdom of God as the imminent end of the world."[23] Jesus probably had some eschatological beliefs and likely believed that God's promises to Israel would someday be fulfilled. For Borg, however, "noneschatological" does not mean that Jesus never said anything about eschatology; it means, "imminent eschatology is not to be the interpretive context for reading the Jesus tradition."[24]

Borg's historical Jesus is a "Spirit-filled person in the charismatic stream of Judaism." Utilizing the work of Geza Vermes, Borg argues that Jesus was similar to other Jewish holy men active primarily in Galilee during this period, such as Honi the Circle-Drawer and Hanina ben Dosa. These holy men mediated the power of the Spirit especially as healers and rainmakers (25–32).[25] It is "virtually indisputable" that Jesus was a healer and exorcist, because those stories have widespread attestation in the earliest sources, such activities were common in the ancient world, and even Jesus' opponents did not challenge this fact. Although we cannot determine the historical accuracy of all the details, we are dealing with "generally historical material" (61). Jesus' exorcisms and healings "were the product of the power which flowed through him as a holy man" (67).[26]

Jesus was deeply involved in the sociopolitical life of his people. The social, political, and economic pressures of Roman occupation generated a cultural crisis and fragmentation among Jews (79–93). Jesus had a multifaceted role within this social world: He was a *sage,* a teacher of an "alternative wisdom" who pointed to a *way of transformation.* This wisdom was a radical criticism of the conventional wisdom of his day—the "ethos of holiness" understood as purity (97). Jesus spoke of a God who was ultimately gracious and compassionate (100), not the God of conventional wisdom who focused on reward and punishment (115). Jesus replaced "Be holy as God is holy" with "Be compassionate as God is compassionate."[27]

Jesus also was a *revitalization movement founder*[28] who wanted to renew Israel with a charismatic, itinerant movement grounded in the Spirit, centered on him, and marked by joy and compassion, especially for the poor, outcasts, and sinners (124–40). Jesus sought to transform his social world by creating an alternative community structured around compassion—inclusiveness, acceptance, love, and peace (142).

Yet of all the figures in his tradition, Borg argues, Jesus is most like the classical prophets of Israel. The whole of Jesus' ministry was a call to repent and turn to God (150, 164). Although the possibility of judgment runs throughout Jesus' warnings, this call to change was viewed as an opportunity, and the overall tone of his ministry was not judgment but joy (165). Jesus did speak of a last judgment, but there is no reason to believe that he thought it was imminent (157).

As the climax of his prophetic mission and call to renewal, Jesus went to Jerusalem to make a final appeal to his people. He chose the symbol from Zechariah 9:9, the king of peace riding on a colt, to make a dramatic prophetic entrance into the city. His second even more dramatic prophetic act was his provocation in the temple. These two prophetic acts symbolized his message of indictment, threat, and call to change; they also led to his execution by Pilate as a political rebel (176, 179). Although historians cannot say exactly what happened next, Jesus' followers continued to experience him as a living reality *"in a new way"*—having the qualities of God: "…Spirit triumphed over culture" (185).

Borg made a distinctive contribution to the discussions, one in which he labored to make Jesus' message and social program understandable in first-century terms and relevant for modern society. Although it was intended for general readers, Borg intentionally addressed his book also to the church so that the historical Jesus could be a "potent source of renewal" (ix).[29]

There is much to praise about Borg's interdisciplinary reconstruction, but—perhaps in his desire to make Jesus more relevant—he downplays the clearly imminent eschatological elements of

Jesus' message. A number of passages, in addition to the future Son of man sayings, indicate Jesus' belief in an imminent end of the world, a continuous thread of expectation that runs from John the Baptist through Jesus to the early church.[30]

Critics of the Jesus Seminar

Reactions to the Jesus Seminar ranged from praise to mockery and personal attacks, but the Seminar provoked serious debates about sources, methodology, and historical perspectives.

The Real Jesus by Luke Timothy Johnson

On a rhetorical level—in the sense that it did not elevate the level of discourse—one of the most disappointing responses to the Jesus Seminar was Luke Timothy Johnson's *The Real Jesus*. On a substantive level, Johnson focused on the limits of historical reconstruction of a "real Jesus" and, on a more fundamental level, questioned its adequacy for "the grounding of Christian faith" (x).

From the very first page, sparks fly as Johnson begins to grind his ax. The content of his response is almost lost in the negative rhetoric he uses to attack the Seminar. The Seminar produced "second-rate scholarship" (xi), its members were "self-selected," spent ten years in "self promotion" and "media manipulation" (1), and participated in a "self-indulgent charade" (26). Funk comes under specific attack for his "entrepreneurship" and "knack for power that is highly personalized" (1–2). Funk, Johnson alleges, is a P. T. Barnum–like "ringmaster-entrepreneur" and "Magister Ludi" (6, 13), whose statements reveal a "strange combination of grandiosity and hucksterism" (8) and who engages in deliberate deception (7).

Other members of the Seminar do not escape Johnson's scorn. Johnson echoes words similar to an earlier essay from Richard Hays[31] and questions the academic credentials of many in the Seminar, since they, in Johnson/Hays's view, "by no means [represent] the cream of New Testament scholarship" (3). When Johnson wrote, no member of the Seminar had a faculty position at Yale, Harvard, Princeton, Duke, or other institutions deemed worthy by Johnson/Hays, and most members were in "relatively undistinguished academic positions" (3). In this condescending response by Johnson/Hays, I almost hear echoes of Nathanael in John 1:46: "Can anything good come out of Nazareth?" These *ad hominem* attacks are disappointing.

Johnson reviews a number of writers and scholars along with the Jesus Seminar and finds six problematic "consistent traits" (54–55):

They reject the canonical gospels as reliable sources for our knowledge of Jesus. Johnson, however, also severely questions the historical reliability of the gospels (e.g., 124). He agrees that the gospels are more religious instruction than historical reconstruction (151), and he argues that even if the gospels "agreed entirely" (which they do not), they still would "yield an extraordinarily limited amount of information" (108–9).

These books shape their portrait of Jesus without reference to other canonical sources such as Paul. Johnson observes that the Jesus Seminar voted Jesus' prohibition of divorce as "gray," despite passing the test of the criterion of dissimilarity and its multiple attestation in Mark, Q, and Paul (1 Cor 7:10; 117). Yet Johnson's own attempt to use other canonical sources results in only seventeen rather meager points about Jesus (121–22).[32]

The mission of Jesus and the Jesus movement is portrayed in terms of a social or cultural critique, not in terms of religious realities. Johnson correctly observes that many modern works on the historical Jesus too facilely utilize their analyses to highlight current social/cultural issues important to them, but he also overlooks the fundamental overlap between religion, politics, and society in the ancient world.

These books reveal a theological agenda and assert that traditional Christian belief is a distortion of the "real Jesus." The books of the Jesus Seminar have an ideological agenda, but so does Johnson's book. Johnson's ideological/theological agenda does not disqualify his book from receiving attention; neither should the Jesus Seminar's agenda disqualify theirs.

The shared premise of these books is that historical knowledge is normative for faith and theology (e.g., the original form of the Jesus movement was better than any of its developments). Although I sympathize with Johnson's dilemma—how to defend church, creed, and canon—in this respect, I am closer to Funk's position in the opening quote of this chapter: I am more interested in what Jesus said about God's kingdom than what Paul said about Jesus the Christ. One important aspect of Johnson's point, though, is that many historical Jesus studies tend to denigrate the early church and highlight its role in distorting the "pristine" message of Jesus.

Even though all but one have "some form of identification with Christianity," the primary allegiance of these historical Jesus scholars is to the academy, not to the church. This criticism—such as Johnson's disparagement of Marcus Borg trying to be "both a critical historian and a builder of Christian faith" (41)—misses the mark. An academic study of the historical Jesus can be, at first, difficult for faith, but, with sustained effort, it should lead to a more authentic, robust, and mature faith.

Johnson also argues that the limitations of the historical method are problematic: There is too little evidence, written by tendentious "insiders," and the result is that historical research of Jesus and the Jesus movement is a "house of cards," a "paper chase, pure and simple" (89, 99).[33]

Johnson rejects complete historical skepticism, however, and offers another method to delineate data about the historical Jesus by attempting to locate "converging lines of evidence" (112). Johnson begins with evidence from outside the New Testament (e.g., Josephus). He moves on to the letters of Paul, Hebrews, and James in the New Testament. Finally, he analyzes patterns in the gospel traditions to see where they correlate with these other sources (e.g., reports of Jesus as a wonder-worker).

He finds that the basic "historical" claims of the Nicene Creed are well supported and that every quest of the historical Jesus begins to have credibility problems when scholars try to push beyond this framework (126–27), an erroneous conclusion, in my view. For Johnson, Christian faith was never based on historical reconstructions of Jesus, even though it always involved some historical claims about Jesus (133–34).

Johnson thus argues that what Jesus said, did, and thought should not be the object of Christian faith. Christian faith is directed to a living person; the "real Jesus" is the resurrected Jesus (141–42): "It is Jesus as risen Lord who is experienced in the assembly of believers, declared by the word of proclamation, encountered in the sacramental meal, addressed by prayers of praise and petition" (145–46). Interestingly, some members of the Jesus Seminar agree, in part, with Johnson's comment:

> The religious and intellectual significance of this historical Jesus is consistently overstated....Neither his teachings, nor his prayers, nor his deeds can claim a central place in contemporary meaning schemes....[S]ignificance for the historical Jesus can be asserted, but it is clearly secondary to the significance of the theological and mythical Jesus(es).[34]

Johnson's book serves as a reminder that historical reconstructions of Jesus are tentative; caution and humility are in order. Nevertheless, as Robert Miller correctly observed, "History is not optional."[35] Unfortunately, Johnson's rhetoric perpetuates the media circus that he decries, his agnosticism about the historical Jesus is discouraging, and his solution is unsatisfying. The fact that all historical reconstructions are tentative does not mean that the effort is not necessary or meaningful.[36]

A Witherington Critique

Although not as strident, Ben Witherington's critique of the Seminar also generates more heat than light.[37] Like Johnson,

Witherington is dependent upon the earlier critique by Richard Hays, and he echoes Hays/Johnson's critique that the Jesus Seminar did not include scholars from "prestigious" institutions. More to the mark is Witherington's criticism about the lack of diversity within the Seminar. Other observations, however, are baffling, such as Witherington's contention that the Seminar was committed to the "social-scientific method and computer science" (43).

Witherington also misrepresents part of the Seminar's methodology. He argues that the criterion of dissimilarity should not be the "ultimate or final litmus test" or the "sole determinant." Once again, Witherington is dependent on Hays, and he overstates the case. It would be more accurate to argue that there was an "overreliance on this criterion" in the Seminar's work (47), which is indeed problematic.

Witherington rejects the Seminar's view that the Gospel of Thomas is independent of the canonical gospels and is concerned that the Seminar downplays such traditions as the controversy dialogues, the pronouncement stories, and the "theological and eschatological matrix" out of which the teaching of Jesus operates. The Seminar, however, rated 40 percent of the pronouncements in the pronouncement stories as authentic.[38] Witherington also admits that "a *few*" of the sayings in Thomas with no canonical parallels may be authentic (49). On the other hand, the Seminar itself concluded that only two of those unparalleled sayings could be rated pink (and none red).[39] Witherington's critique again misses the mark in significant ways.

Witherington expresses surprise that the "two things Jesus certainly spoke about" hardly surface in the Seminar's discussions: the "Son of Man" and "kingdom of God" (55). This critique also is misleading, because the Seminar did place emphasis upon these two things—especially the latter—but it reached vastly different conclusions about them than does Witherington. The primary issue for Witherington, though, is a defense of the reliability of the gospels, and he objects to the fact that some scholars "assume they know better than the early

Christians" what Jesus was likely to have said. That assumption, Witherington declares, "is founded on hubris" (48). To the contrary, that "assumption" is based on evidence that is clearly seen when the various gospel stories are placed side-by-side and carefully compared. The problem is inherent in the texts themselves: their varying portraits of Jesus and their different reports of Jesus' words and deeds. Witherington's critique, it seems to me, suffers from the same problem that he finds in the Jesus Seminar. His presuppositions predetermine the Jesus he reconstructs; his "standards" actually are theological presuppositions that demand a "Jesus that will preach" (57).

Witherington's own reconstruction of Jesus is that of a sage, the "embodiment of Wisdom" (185). Jesus was a healer, a prophet, referred to himself as the Son of man, and "saw himself in some sort of messianic light" (185). Witherington also argues that when Jesus says, "Wisdom is vindicated by her deeds" (Matt 11:16–19/Luke 7:31–35), he is talking about himself: Jesus is "acting out the part of Wisdom" (188) and sees himself as a revealer of the very mind of God (e.g., Matt 11:25–27). Wisdom has this role in such scriptures as Proverbs 1, 3, and 8, so Witherington concludes that Jesus thus saw himself as God's Wisdom incarnate.

This reconstruction of Jesus is limited and problematic. Is the fact that Jesus uttered sapiential sayings evidence for Jesus' belief that he was God's Wisdom incarnate? Numerous scholars portray Jesus as some type of sage, but Jesus' *identification* with Wisdom is not supported by the evidence, and it also depends on sayings of debatable authenticity (e.g., Matt 11:25–27).

"Five Gospels but No Gospel": N. T. Wright

N. T. Wright's major review of the Seminar evokes some of the same "gentle mockery" that he finds in most other responses to the Seminar's work.[40] For example, he chides Seminar members for not "turning the other cheek" with their critics, even though that saying "received the rare accolade of a red vote" (84).

Wright commends the scholarly contributions of many members of the Seminar, such as Robert Funk, John Dominic Crossan, James Robinson, Marcus Borg, Bruce Chilton, Walter Wink, Ron Cameron, and John Kloppenborg, but he laments the lack of interaction with other important historical Jesus scholars, such as E. P. Sanders (87). Although Wright unfortunately segues into the same elitist critique about Seminar members not teaching at "prestigious" institutions, he correctly observes that these scholars represent a "very narrow band among contemporary readers of the Gospels" (89). In Wright's view, the stridently "antifundamentalist" agenda of several members of the project tends to lead to a "shallow polarization," and he postulates that some (leading) members of the Seminar were attempting to "exorcize the memory of a strict fundamentalist background" (90).

Wright's critique of the color-coded voting system includes an analysis of how the votes were tabulated. The vote on the parable of the Two Sons illustrates the problem: Fifty-eight percent voted red or pink, but the (minority of) gray and black votes pulled the weighted average into the gray category. Wright concludes: "A voting system that produces a result like this ought to be scrapped" (95).

Wright claims that the Seminar's thirty-six rules of evidence, in practice, boil down to three "guiding principles":

(1) *A majority of the Fellows began with the presupposition that Jesus was a traveling sage and wonder-worker* (98). Wright accuses the Seminar of having a predetermined shallow and one-dimensional image of Jesus in their "mind all along" (100). I am not a mind reader, so I cannot determine what was in "mind all along," but an examination of the written evidence paints a more nuanced portrait. From the beginning, influential members such as Mack, Crossan, and Borg had already arrived at certain conclusions based on their previous scholarly work. If one reads the papers for the various Seminar meetings, however, one can see

that their various arguments are forcefully and carefully presented. In the end—and after some members with different perspectives dropped out—their position prevailed.

(2) *The Seminar adopts a particular and highly misleading position about eschatology and apocalyptic*. Wright argues that previous attempts to deny Jesus' apocalyptic message were done for apologetic motives: If Jesus predicted the end of the world, he was wrong, so the error was blamed on later Christians. The Jesus Seminar, however, wants to undercut the contemporary apocalyptic preaching of modern fundamentalist movements (101). Wright therefore argues that earlier flights from apocalyptic were designed to "save" orthodox Christianity, whereas the Seminar's efforts are designed to subvert it.

The most important question Wright asks, though, is, how does the Seminar know that Jesus preached a nonapocalyptic message, when it admits that apocalyptic ideas "were everywhere in the air" (102)? That key question deserves further investigation. Wright instead, however, takes his own flight from apocalyptic—perhaps in his own attempt to "save" orthodox Christianity—by declaring that apocalyptic language was not meant to be taken literally; it was a "complex metaphor-system" through which many ancient Jews expressed their aspirations for "social, political and above all theological liberation" (103). With this move Wright can (attempt to) preserve the apocalyptic message of Jesus without admitting that Jesus was wrong about the end of the world's imminence. Wright's position, however, is just as difficult to maintain as the nonapocalyptic Jesus position.

(3) *The Seminar assumes a particular image of the early church with regard to the transmission of material about Jesus.* It assumes that only isolated sayings about Jesus circulated in the post-Easter period (111). Wright counters by arguing that communities in oral cultures tell the same stories over and over again. In the process, these stories acquire a fairly fixed form: "They retain that form, and phraseology, as long as they are told" (113). The storyteller in such a culture "has no license" to invent or

adapt at will, especially with a story that is important to the community. A story about Jesus healing someone, for example, would acquire a fixed form within the first two or three retellings and retain that form, "other things being equal" (114).

Although it is clear that the Jesus Seminar ascribes too much invention of material to early Christians, Wright's scenario appears to be not much more than wishful thinking. A close, comparative reading of the various stories about Jesus in the gospels is enough to rebut this argument about a fixed form, although Wright's language carefully includes some loopholes (e.g., "other things being equal").

Wright concludes by saying that he is grateful for the Seminar's publishing of Jesus material from canonical and noncanonical sources, but he regrets the "close-minded" hatred of orthodoxy. In addition, popularization of scholarship is not in itself a bad thing, but the Seminar wrongly publicizes itself as the bearer of the "assured result of scholarship" (118). The result is that the Seminar is "culpably irresponsible," because it misleads nonscholars about Jesus and the state of "serious scholarship." Wright agrees that the search for Jesus in his historical context is "possible, vital, and urgent" (119), but the way to approach this context is not to divide the material up into bits and then to vote on them one by one.

N. T. Wright's Reconstruction

Wright's complex and voluminous works stem from his belief that "serious study of Jesus and the gospels is best done within the context of a worshipping community."[41] *The New Testament and the People of God,* for example, sets the context for his portrait of Jesus in his *Jesus and the Victory of God.*[42] His theory of interpretation, *critical realism,* places Jesus in the context of first-century Palestinian Judaism but builds a bridge from the first-century historical Jesus to twenty-first-century "orthodoxy."[43]

Wright believes that the synoptic gospels, despite their wide divergences, share a common pattern. The authors did not recount "bare facts" without interpretation, but the telling of these stories depends upon "unique and unrepeatable events which had taken place earlier" (398). The gospels place Jesus' story in the form of the history of Israel in miniature; the typology of Israel's story is now Jesus' story (401–2).

Although Wright recognizes the pluriformity of first-century Judaism (118), he sees an "authentic first-century Jewish world-view" (149). The pressing need of most first-century Jews had to do with liberation from oppression, from debt, and from Rome (169). They envisioned themselves as "god's" (per Wright's usage) chosen people, in the holy land, focused on the temple but still in exile (243). Most Jews, Wright argues, believed that God would act to "restore [Israel's] fortunes" and end their "exile" (280). This exile is not a geographical exile, but "a period of history with certain characteristics": They were not living in their ideal world, and their God was committed to bring about their liberation.[44]

Wright believes that expectations of this deliverance were often expressed metaphorically through apocalyptic language. The "human figure" in Daniel 7, for example, functions as a symbol that Israel, although beleaguered and battered, is about to be vindicated (292). But within these Jewish writings *"there is virtually no evidence that Jews were expecting the end of the space-time universe."* They "knew a good metaphor when they saw one," and they used this cosmic imagery to illustrate the significance of socio-political events. The *"present world order"* would come to an end, and Israel would be vindicated (333–34).[45]

Jesus and the Victory of God argues that Jesus retold Israel's stories in new but comprehensible ways, spoke and acted prophetically, and told his hearers that their restoration was at hand. Jesus saw himself as charged by God to regroup Israel around himself and to return from exile. Jesus' counter-temple movement aroused hostility from both the temple authorities and the Romans, and this led to his death. Jesus was vindicated by his resurrection, however, and his followers continued to believe that the kingdom had arrived. Therefore, the gospels retell the original story of Israel with an eye to this new, but theologically consistent, setting (132).

For example, Wright's (unlikely) interpretation of the parable of the Two Sons (Luke 15:11–32) is that it symbolizes the story of Israel—its exile to "a distant country" and restoration with the Father. The exodus is the ultimate backdrop; exile and restoration constitute the central drama that "Israel believed herself to be acting out," and the parable of the Prodigal Son says that this hope is now being fulfilled (127).

Wright's confidence in the reliability of the tradition is reflected by his use of the "criterion of double similarity (and dissimilarity)": When something can be seen as credible (even if subversive) within first-century Judaism *and* credible as the implied starting point (but not a replica) of something in early Christianity, there "is a strong possibility of our being in touch with the genuine history of Jesus" (132). Examples would include Jesus' shocking attitude toward his family and his inclusive table fellowship (149). Wright also believes that although there was some flexibility in the oral tradition, the whole community knew the tradition well enough to prevent serious innovation (134). These two—overly optimistic, in my view—assumptions essentially shift the burden of proof from those who must demonstrate authenticity to those who wish to argue that a saying is inauthentic.

The Praxis of a Prophet. For Wright, the best initial model for Jesus is as a prophet bearing an urgent eschatological/apocalyptic message for Israel (150). Both his sayings and deeds evoked contemporary pictures of prophetic activity. This public persona, however, was insufficient to do justice to the disciples' developing perceptions of Jesus, because Jesus believed that he was inaugurating the kingdom and bringing Israel's history to its climax (197).

Jesus' Aims and Beliefs. For Wright, Jesus saw himself as the focal point of the returning-from-exile Israel. He was the true interpreter of the Torah, the true builder of the new, restored temple, and the true spokesperson for Wisdom. He also was the king through whom YHWH was restoring Israel, although not a king as the Hasmoneans or Herodians. In his redefinition of his role as the Messiah, Jesus felt called by God to *evoke* the traditions promising YHWH's return, *enact* those traditions in Jerusalem, and thereby *embody* YHWH's return. The kingdom was coming in and through his work and would be accomplished through suffering (651–52).

The result, after the resurrection, was that the early Christians celebrated the victory of Jesus over evil as something that had already happened. That was the basis of their "remarkable joy," as well as the subject of Wright's next book, *The Resurrection of the Son of God,* in which he argues that the empty tomb and Jesus' appearances were actual events, not creations of the early church: "The proposal that Jesus was bodily raised from the dead possesses unrivalled power to explain the historical data at the heart of early Christianity."[46]

Although Wright's volumes challenge some naïve and dogmatic traditionalist assumptions, they are written from within a traditional Christian perspective primarily for those readers who share most of his religious views.[47] His signal contribution to traditional, conservative scholarship is that his conclusions allow him to affirm those gospel traditions that portray Jesus as an apocalyptic prophet but to do so in a way that also allows Jesus to succeed—not incorrectly to predict an imminent end of the world. The convenience of this discovery makes one look askance at this result and raise serious questions about its veracity.

Another problematic presupposition is Wright's view that the more evidence from the synoptic gospels that he can fit into his portrait of Jesus the better. Obviously, this assumption depends upon the authenticity of the evidence that is included. Wright presents this presupposition as a conclusion from the evidence,[48] but it clearly is a (debatable if not questionable) presupposition. Like many other scholars, Wright ignores evidence that many developments within the synoptic tradition are due to deliberate changes.

Did the Jews still feel themselves to be in exile? This theory and the interpretations related to it appear dubious.[49] Wright's portrait preserves in a creative and innovative way many of the traditional ideas about Jesus as Messiah, but his answers and his metanarrative of a "return from exile" are ultimately unconvincing.

Conclusion

One of the most even-handed assessments of the Jesus Seminar's work is found in Mark Allan Powell's *Jesus as a Figure in History*.[50] He categorizes several criticisms leveled against the Seminar, and I will build upon his observations.

Many of the criticisms of the Seminar are to a large extent *ad hominem* attacks that sometimes impugn their honesty and integrity. Critics, beginning with Richard Hays, find fault with the Seminar's motives, tactics, and membership. Members of the Seminar are portrayed as "lapsed Christians," who set out to avenge the damage that fundamentalists had inflicted upon them in earlier years. The ways in which the Seminar utilized the media and brought scholarship into the public arena have also dismayed some critics.

Aside from the flamboyant and provocative words of Robert Funk and some others, what is inherently wrong with public discussions of scholarship? Not surprisingly, the Seminar voted as "pink" Jesus' words in Luke 11:33: "No one lights a lamp and then puts it in a cellar or under a bushel basket, but rather on a lampstand so that those who come in can see the light." The "light" generated by the Seminar may be faint or dim, but providing the public with scholarly information seems to me to be an ethical stance: Is it altogether a bad thing to offer an alternative point of view among the current media and political dominance of

the "right-wing Christian community"?[51] The lack of diversity of
Seminar membership is a problem, but the academic snobbery of
Hays and others who followed him is disheartening. The Seminar's ideological slant, however, is clear—especially after conservative members of the Seminar—such as Southern Baptists
feeling their denomination's pressure—dropped out. The emer-
gence of the nonapocalyptic Jesus also led some members to drop
out. As Powell notes, the Seminar thus is "representative of one
voice within the [New Testament] guild, a voice that actually
espouses a minority position on some key issues" (78).

More germane are criticisms of the Seminar's methodology,
results, and interpretations of the data. Many scholars still use the
criterion of dissimilarity, for example, but not to the extent of the
Seminar, and many appropriately question the lack of continuity
the Seminar envisions between the eschatological views of John
the Baptist, Jesus, and early Christianity.[52] More questions can be
raised about the independence of the Gospel of Thomas and the
reliability and use of the reconstructions of the various "levels" of
Q—or even whether the existence of Q itself is a valid hypothesis.[53] The charge by critics of the Seminar about "predetermined
results" is a problem, but the problem is not as simple as many
critics suggest—that (influential) members already had their
minds made up about Jesus before starting this quest. Instead, the
main issue is one of methodology. How the Seminar began
methodologically influenced greatly where it went. The decisions
about Q and the Gospel of Thomas, for example, determined the
course of many decisions about the authenticity of sayings, as well
as the content and style of Jesus' teaching. The Seminar's
approach of examining independently circulated sayings also is a
major methodological weakness. The dialogical relations of these
sayings—with each other, with the situations in which they were
uttered, and the actions with which the words are connected—
exhibit much of the nature of the entire aphoristic tradition attributed to Jesus.[54] The use of the Gospel of Thomas and the
reconstruction of an earlier layer of Q, combined with the criterion

of dissimilarity, helped to create its view of Jesus as a noneschato-logical sage, which led some critics to charge that the Seminar produced a "non-Jewish Jesus." As Robert Miller noted, however, the "Jewishness of Jesus is a phony issue."[55] The real question is what type of Jew Jesus was.

The Jesus Seminar worked as a collaborative group in a distinctive fashion, something unusual in scholarship even today. I differ with it in matters of style, substance, and conclusions, but the Seminar made a significant contribution to scholarly and public dialogues.

4
The Eschatological Prophet and the Restoration of Israel

> Jesus thought that God would soon bring about a decisive change in the world. This context is historically crucial, since it is the framework of Jesus' overall mission: it includes the man who baptized him, and also his own followers.[1]

E. P. Sanders cemented his reputation as an expert on first-century Judaism with his masterful book *Paul and Palestinian Judaism*.[2] That book argued that *covenantal nomism* was consistently found in Jewish literature from early second century BCE to late second century CE and that it was *pervasive* in Palestine before 70 CE (426–28). *Covenantal nomism* presupposes God's loyalty to the covenant with Israel and, in most expressions, the expectation that Israel's response of gratitude and faith would include showing loyalty by obeying God's law.[3] Sanders envisions covenantal nomism as the common denominator for virtually all varieties of Judaism. In his two books on the historical Jesus, Sanders places Jesus firmly within covenantal nomism and explores how Jesus operated within the Judaism of his day.

Jesus and Judaism

In this work, Sanders examines how Jesus could live totally within Judaism yet be the origin, in some sense, of a movement that separated from Judaism.

The Restoration of Israel

Sanders argues that one should begin with what is relatively secure and work out to more uncertain points. Disagreements arrive, however, when one explicitly states which words and/or deeds are "relatively secure" or establishes ground rules for identifying them (3). In addition, the numerous investigations of Jesus' sayings assumed that Jesus primarily was a "teacher" and have not yielded "a convincing historical depiction of Jesus" (5). The sayings of Jesus thus play a secondary but important role in Sanders's reconstruction. Unfortunately, Sanders often does not provide detailed discussions of why he finds a saying to be authentic or inauthentic, even though he believes that the burden of proof should fall on the one who argues a case (13). He attempts to bypass this objection, however, by beginning with "facts" about Jesus, which he believes will help explain why Jesus attracted attention, why he was executed, and why he was subsequently deified (7).

Sanders builds his case upon the following "almost indisputable facts" (11):
1. John the Baptist baptized Jesus.
2. Jesus was a Galilean who preached and healed.
3. Jesus called disciples and spoke of there being twelve.
4. Jesus confined his activity to Israel.
5. Jesus engaged in controversy about the temple.
6. Jesus was crucified by Roman authorities.
7. After his death, Jesus' followers continued as an identifiable movement.

8. At least some Jews persecuted at least parts of the new movement.

Sanders begins with the temple controversy, because he believes "our information is a little better" about it, and because it can be "isolated in some degree" from other questions (11–12). One problem is that he must utilize sayings of Jesus about the destruction of the temple that are of debatable authenticity. Sanders denies that these sayings are *vaticinium ex eventu,* prophecy after the event (73), and argues that despite the problems, it is "overwhelmingly probable that Jesus did something in the temple and said something about its destruction" (61). Sanders then situates Jesus within "restoration eschatology":[4] Jesus publicly predicted or threatened the imminent destruction of the temple and probably awaited the establishment of a new temple from heaven (71). The end was at hand, the temple would be destroyed, and the new and perfect temple would soon arise (75). Most of the things we know about Jesus with "virtually complete certainty" place him in the category of a prophet of Jewish restoration, such as Jesus' calling of twelve apostles, which points to the hope for the restoration of the twelve tribes of Israel (103).

In order to substantiate this hypothesis about Jesus' restoration theology, Sanders seeks to demonstrate that the idea of the restoration of Israel, including a new temple, was current in some circles of first-century Judaism. Although such expectations are neither "universal" nor "clear and consistent" (87), the theme of a new temple appears in several different places.

Yet Sanders also admits that Jesus' message is distinct from other expectations of restoration. His message "curiously lacks emphasis on one of the most important themes"—a message of repentance to escape punishment at the judgment. Jesus most likely believed in repentance, but there is no firm tradition that shows that he issued a call for national repentance in view of the coming end (110).

The Kingdom

Beyond a doubt, Sanders notes, Jesus proclaimed the kingdom (ruling power) of God. It is also beyond doubt that Jesus attached special significance to his own career and saw it as intimately connected to the kingdom. It is possible that Jesus saw the kingdom as breaking in with his own words and deeds, but scholars have overemphasized this aspect to make Jesus' message "more relevant" and "distinctive" (154). The evidence indicates that Jesus expected a future and imminent kingdom, one that assumes that a decisive future event will result in a recognizable social order involving Jesus' disciples and presumably Jesus himself.

Jesus' teaching about the kingdom was distinctive, Sanders argues, because he included sinners—those wicked persons who defied God's law by refusing to renounce their sins and repent (174). Jesus' "offense" was proclaiming that the wicked were included in the kingdom without requiring repentance—restitution, sacrifice, and afterward obeying the law (206). This distinctive view of his own mission—that participation in the kingdom of God was guaranteed to those who accepted him—would be offensive to most of his fellow Jews. It also indicates that Jesus saw himself as having an exalted role in that kingdom.

Conflict and Death

Sanders questions the assumption that Jesus consciously challenged the adequacy of the Mosaic law. Instead, Sanders argues that the gesture in the temple symbolized the end of the old order and the coming of a new one. It demonstrates, however, that Jesus viewed the current Mosaic dispensation as not the final one (252). A new, better one was imminent.

Besides the conflict over the temple, the most revealing passage for understanding Jesus' view of the law is "Let the dead bury the dead" (e.g., Matt 8:22). There are no parallels to this statement in Judaism or the wider Hellenistic-Roman world, and it conflicts with Mosaic law and Hellenistic-Roman piety. The statement has a positive thrust—an urgent call to discipleship that overrides all other responsibilities—and a negative one: disobeying God's requirement to care for one's dead parents. Jesus thus consciously requires disobedience of a commandment understood by all Jews to have been given by God (253–54), so at least once Jesus said that following him superseded the requirements of piety and the Torah. This suggests, once again, that "Jesus was prepared, if necessary, to challenge the adequacy of the Mosaic dispensation" (255).

On the other hand, Sanders argues that Jesus' controversies with Pharisees in the gospels reflect later debates between Judaism and Christianity; Sanders doubts that there were any substantial points of opposition between Jesus and the Pharisees over the Sabbath, food, and purity laws (264–65). In fact, the gospels portray "no actual transgression of the law on the part of Jesus" (besides the demand to let the dead bury the dead), but they also give evidence that Jesus did not think that the Mosaic law was "final or absolutely binding," because the new age was at hand (267).

On this point, does Sanders domesticate Jesus? Sanders would respond that portrayals of Pharisees as hypocritical legalists are domestications that trivialize Jesus' message to make it more relevant for today's churches (279). Although I do not completely agree with Sanders's position, his arguments are a needed corrective to the often-caricatured view of first-century Judaism that is found in some New Testament scholarship even today.

Sanders concludes that Jesus came into conflict with views, opinions, and convictions of most Jews through his threatening words and actions against the temple and his promise that sinners would be in the kingdom of God. Anyone who claimed to speak for God and who attracted a following would alarm people who wanted to maintain the "somewhat precarious *status quo* with Rome" (288).

The Romans executed Jesus as would-be "king of the Jews," and his followers later formed a messianic movement that was not based on any hope of military victory (194). Jesus was allegedly executed as king, Sanders notes, but his followers were not rounded up and executed. Thus neither Jesus nor his disciples were perceived to constitute any real threat to Rome. Jesus was dangerous because he excited the hopes and dreams of others but was not a leader of an insurgent group (295).

Jesus made two public, symbolic gestures that led to his death: entering Jerusalem on a donkey and overturning the tables of the moneychangers in the temple (227). His entry into Jerusalem symbolically proclaimed his special role in God's kingdom; God would bring in the kingdom miraculously and would vindicate Jesus' message (235).

The *physical demonstration* in the temple and his *noticeable following* led the Romans to consider Jesus as a threat to public order. Sanders deems these two points critical: Jesus did more than just speak against the temple, and he had enough followers to make it expedient to kill him (302–3). No one misunderstood the threat posed by Jesus: The minor disturbance in the temple, the physical demonstration against it, and a noticeable following led immediately to Jesus' death (305).

Jesus taught about the *kingdom;* he was executed as would-be *king;* and his disciples, after his death, expected him to return to establish the *kingdom*. These points, Sanders declares, are "indisputable," and we should accept the obvious: Jesus' self-claim was great indeed, and it is "by no means unlikely" that he thought of himself as God's "viceroy-to-be" (240). Jesus also gave himself and his disciples roles in the kingdom (307). His role was superior, and it could be summarized as "king," albeit a humble one (309). This possibly led to discussions of him as Messiah in his lifetime and definitely led to this title being ascribed to him after the resurrection. The Jewish aristocrats and the Romans were not mistaken; they clearly understood that what Jesus did was *tantamount* to claiming kingship (322).

Jesus and Judaism: Conclusions

Sanders admits that he does not have all the answers, but he does offer his evaluations of the historically "certain" to the virtually "impossible" elements about Jesus:

I. Certain or virtually certain
   a. Jesus shared the worldview of Jewish restoration eschatology.
   b. He preached the kingdom of God.
   c. He promised the kingdom to the wicked.
   d. He did not explicitly oppose the law (e.g., Sabbath and food).
   e. Neither he nor his disciples thought that the kingdom would be established by the force of arms. They looked for an eschatological miracle.

II. Highly probable
   a. The kingdom he expected had some analogies with this world: leaders, twelve tribes, and a functioning temple.
   b. Jesus' disciples thought of him as king, and he accepted the role, either implicitly or explicitly.

III. Probable
   a. He thought that the wicked who accepted his message would share in the kingdom even though they did not make the customary atonement for sin.
   b. He did not emphasize the national character of the kingdom, including judgment and mass repentance, because John the Baptist, whose work Jesus accepted, accomplished that task.
   c. Jesus spoke of the kingdom in different contexts and used the term in various ways and with multiple nuances.

IV. Possible
   a. He may have spoken of the kingdom in the visionary manner of Mark 13's "little apocalypse" and/or as a present reality into which individuals can enter.

V. Conceivable
   a. He may have thought that the kingdom, in all its power and might, was present in his words and deeds.
   b. He may have given his death martyrological significance.
   c. He may have identified himself with a cosmic Son of man and conceived his attaining kingship in that way.

VI. Incredible
   a. He was one of the rare Jews of his day who believed in love, mercy, grace, repentance, and the forgiveness of sins.
   b. Jews in general, and Pharisees in particular, would kill people who believed in such things.
   c. Because of his work, Jewish confidence in election was "shaken to pieces," and Judaism as a religion was destroyed.

This mode of categorization is strikingly similar to the Jesus Seminar's fourfold ranking of the sayings and actions of Jesus—albeit with significant differences in form, method, content, and results.

Sanders recognizes that his reconstruction of the historical Jesus will not be particularly relevant to Christian faith and practice, but he does not venture into that "theological problem" (327).[5] He notes that he has long been engaged "in the effort to free history and exegesis from the control of theology"; he does not want to reach conclusions that are "pre-determined by theological commitment" (334).

Control is the key word. One's ideology always influences one's approach, methodology, and conclusions, but an acknowledgement of that ideology, as well as an effort to see beyond it, can help to assure that it will not have a determinative influence or control on one's conclusions. In many ways, Sanders's reconstruction of Jesus does not fit his own ideological perspective:

> I am a liberal, modern, secularized Protestant, brought up in a church dominated by low Christology and the social gospel. I am proud of the things that the religious tradition stands for. I am not bold enough, however, to suppose that Jesus came to establish it, or that he died for the sake of its principles (334).

In other respects, though, Sanders's reconstruction serves as a vigorous defense of covenantal nomism, a theory which actually may be, for him, a more important ideological position than his "liberal Protestantism" when it comes to reconstructing the life and teachings of Jesus. Perhaps that also is one reason why Sanders incorrectly downplays Jesus' proclamation of repentance.

The Historical Figure of Jesus

Sanders begins *The Historical Figure of Jesus* by noting that books about Jesus are harder to write than books about other historical figures. Virtually all people have their own view of Jesus—usually favorable, since they want to agree with Jesus, or, more precisely, they want Jesus to agree with them! This favorable view of Jesus begins, of course, with the gospels themselves (6–7), so the historian has to subject the gospels to "rough handling" (xiii). Historians cannot choose only the parts of the gospels that are noble or that can inspire others, because historians try to determine what can be proved, what disproved, and what lies in between (8).

Sanders begins with a similar list of "facts" about Jesus (cf. *Jesus and Judaism*) that are "almost beyond dispute." Some items notably deleted from his earlier list are the healing activity of Jesus (mentioned later), the calling of the Twelve, and the explicit mention that his activity was confined to Israel. There are, however, some additions to the list—"equally secure facts" about what occurred after Jesus' death:

- his disciples first fled;
- they saw him (in what sense is not certain) after his death;
- as a consequence, they believed that he would return to found the kingdom;
- they formed a community to await his return and sought to win others to faith in him as God's Messiah (11).

Historical Contexts

Sanders recognizes the difficulties of reconstructing the historical Jesus but is confident that once the words and contexts are known, "we shall know a lot about Jesus" (77). The events immediately preceding and following Jesus' ministry, for example, give us significant insights. John the Baptist expected a dramatic, imminent event that would change the present order. Jesus, who was baptized by John, apparently agreed that it was time to repent in light of the coming wrath and redemption (94). The expectation of an imminent act of God is also found in the early Christian church (e.g., 1 Thess 4:13–17). Therefore, Sanders argues, the only reasonable explanation is that Jesus taught his followers that God would soon bring about a decisive change in the world.

The Setting of Jesus' Ministry

The village of Capernaum on the northern coast of the Sea of Galilee seems to have been the center for Jesus' ministry. Fishing dominated Capernaum's economy, and according to the gospels, Jesus worked among his "own": fishermen, minor artisans, tradesmen, and farmers. The woes on Capernaum, Bethsaida, and Chorazin, however, indicate some tension between Jesus and the seaside villages (103).

Jesus and his disciples were itinerant; as they moved from village to village, they found individuals willing to provide a meal and simple lodging. Jesus probably led an impoverished life during his active career. He was essentially homeless with minimal financial resources, although he was sometimes able to eat and sleep in comfort because of some supporters, including women (109–11).

Sanders interprets Jesus' calling of twelve disciples as evidence that he envisioned the full restoration of the people of Israel by an eschatological miracle of God. Jesus' fame, though, resulted from his healings and exorcisms, and he probably saw these miracles in an eschatological context: The new age was at hand, and he was fulfilling the hopes of the prophets (168). He also thought that in the very near future God would dramatically intervene in history by sending the Son of man. Although many scholars would like to make these passages disappear, these sayings are "the most securely attested tradition" (182), and they cohere with the eschatological expectations of John the Baptist and the early church. Since Jesus expected that God was going to change human society in the immediate future, it is unlikely that "the main thrust of Jesus' career was social reform" (188). Jesus expected a "new and better age," but he probably spoke about how that new age would be and urged people to live appropriately.

In my view, Sanders underestimates Jesus' prophetic critique of the social and economic oppression of the peasants by the first-century elite. Not all of Jesus' message was generated from or determined by a belief in the imminent end, and even if it were, his view of the future life in the coming kingdom would certainly have significant implications—more than Sanders seems to acknowledge—for the life one lives in the present.

Jesus' View of His Role in God's Plan

Sanders portrays Jesus as a kind and generous man who likely expected some Gentiles to participate in the coming kingdom (192). The overall tenor of his message is compassion towards human frailty, and most of his ethical teaching involves treating other human beings justly, with love and compassion. People should be perfect, but God was lenient, and Jesus displayed God's mercy by being gentle and loving towards others, including sinners (204).

Sanders restates his view that people would have taken offense at Jesus' associating with tax collectors and sinners and his command to "let the dead bury the dead." Jesus' message was radical, because he apparently thought that the "wicked" who followed him, although they technically had not repented in the way the law required, would be included in God's kingdom. Jesus believed that God was acting through him, directly and immediately, bypassing the biblically sanctioned ordinances and reaching out to the lost sheep of Israel (236–37). Jesus thus claimed the authority to speak and act on God's behalf. Although Sanders thinks it unlikely that Jesus claimed the title of Messiah for himself, his actual claim may have been higher. God was king, but Jesus was God's viceroy who represented God both in his ministry and in the coming kingdom (247).

Jesus' Last Week

Sanders postulates that when Jesus rode into Jerusalem on a donkey, he most likely decided to fulfill the prophecy in Zechariah 9:9 and implicitly declared himself to be king. His followers understood, and they hailed the coming kingdom. Second, Jesus' action in the temple and his words against it created deep offense. He thought that God was about to destroy the temple, create a new age, reassemble the twelve tribes of Israel, and build a new and perfect temple (261). Third, Jesus' last meal with the disciples symbolically pointed to the future kingdom. By that time, Jesus probably knew that he was a marked man. He went to the Mount of Olives to pray and wait for the reaction of the authorities and possibly the intervention of God. He hoped that he would not die, but he resigned himself to the will of God.

Jesus' prophetic demonstration in the temple was the immediate cause of his arrest and death. Caiaphas recommended to Pilate that Jesus be executed, and Pilate—having heard that Jesus thought he was king of the Jews—most likely had Jesus flogged, briefly interrogated, and then sent to the cross without a second thought. After a relatively short period of suffering, Jesus died, and some of his followers hastily buried him (274–75).

As Sanders notes, what happened next was a surprise. Jesus' followers became convinced that he rose from the dead: "That Jesus' followers (and later Paul) had resurrection experiences is, in my judgement, a fact. What the reality was that gave rise to the experiences I do not know" (280). His followers believed this, they lived it, and they died for it.

Reactions to Sanders's Reconstruction

Jesus and Judaism won the Louisville Grawemeyer Award in Religion (1990) as the best book in religion in the 1980's. Similarly, the *London Correspondent* named it as one of the two most important works on religious history written in the 1980's. Likewise, *The Historical Figure of Jesus* is brilliantly written and cogently argued. The Jesus Seminar dominated the headlines, but many scholars were (re)affirming aspects of the eschatological Jesus.

Sanders's *historical* Jesus, though, largely reflects the *synoptic* Jesus. As a perusal of his "Index of Passages" in both books demonstrates, Sanders utilizes no noncanonical texts, and he ignores, for the most part, the Gospel of John. Sanders's approach is distinctive, however, because he begins with a "list of facts" about Jesus rather than sayings ascribed to him.

Most scholars consider the majority of these "facts" to be bedrock traditions about Jesus. Some exceptions occur, such as John Dominic Crossan's claim that the "Twelve" was a later creation of the church,[6] but most items on Sanders's lists are noncontroversial. Difficulties arise, however, when Sanders moves from fact to interpretation: It is one thing to say, "Jesus did something in the temple," and quite another to claim that Jesus' overturning of the tables in the temple symbolized its destruction and restoration.[7] The first recounts an event; the second attempts to discern the intention behind that event, and differences of opinion begin to multiply. Sanders then takes an additional step by situating Jesus' actions (and words) into an interpretive framework: Jewish restoration theology. That assumption allows Sanders to claim that Jesus' action in the temple symbolically proclaims *both* destruction *and* restoration. Here Sanders seems to go beyond the definitive evidence. As Dale Allison aptly notes, "The turning over of the tables in the temple is…less an illuminating episode than an episode that needs to be illuminated."[8] Yet Jesus' appointment of the Twelve indicates that he expected the eschatological restoration of the twelve tribes of Israel.[9] Even though Sanders prioritizes Jesus' actions, however, these actions do not occur in an interpretive vacuum; they are evaluated in light of Jesus' words. As John Meier observes, Sanders's interpretation of Jesus' actions in the temple would be very weak indeed if he did not also utilize Jesus' sayings that prophesy the temple's destruction.[10]

Other scholars have raised objections about how Jesus could proclaim an acute eschatological crisis and produce parables that display a sapiential (i.e., wisdom) base. Marcus Borg, for example, noted that wisdom is central to the Jesus tradition, and he could not reconcile the image of Jesus as a prophet of restoration theology with the large body of data suggesting that he was a teacher of subversive wisdom.[11] In my view, this apparent dichotomy is a false one. Amos Wilder, for example, argued that Jesus united these disparate elements of wisdom and eschatology into his teaching.[12] John Kloppenborg also noted that several wisdom texts from

Qumran display elements of future eschatology, as does the Wisdom of Solomon.[13] Sapiential and eschatological elements are not mutually exclusive. In fact, they can go hand in hand, because they function similarly—to deny the validity of the status quo.[14]

Sanders, however, overestimates the tension between eschatological and sapiential elements in a way that leads him not only to downplay many parables and aphorisms but also to underestimate Jesus' social critique. Sanders also, incorrectly in my view, downplays the tensions between cities and villages, as well as the elite and nonelite, which means that he neglects important implications for how Jesus, a peasant artisan, would respond to such oppression. A more holistic view of restoration eschatology includes God's comprehensive righting of wrongs, where the world "will be utterly, completely, and irrevocably changed."[15] Jesus envisioned a new set of power relations in the eschatological kingdom, and this view inherently included social dimensions—a vision of how this new society will function—which has immediate and clear demands for the present.[16]

Sometimes Sanders uses the criterion of dissimilarity; sometimes he does not. We cannot assume *a priori* either that Jesus' teachings were discontinuous with Judaism—the first half of the criterion of dissimilarity, but we also cannot assume that he was necessarily in agreement with first-century Judaism(s). Marcus Borg questioned, for example, whether Sanders's Jesus, who operated within Jewish law, had any "significant points of tension" between himself and his Jewish contemporaries.[17] Sanders makes important observations about the implicit and explicit anti-Judaism inherent in much New Testament scholarship, but that perspective may have caused him to downplay the disagreements Jesus had with his contemporaries. If Jesus were willing to say, "Let the dead bury the dead," does that not imply that he could have found exceptions to the law in other instances in light of the eschatological crisis?

Sanders also skirts issues that other scholars deem important. He refuses to devote much time, for example, to the titles ascribed to Jesus, because "we have better information" (Jesus' actions) that will give us more conclusive answers. In addition, Sanders does not enter into many complex exegetical questions and often does not provide enough information as to why he dismisses certain traditions as inauthentic.

Finally, Sanders does not address the theological problem that his portrait of Jesus creates for modern Christianity or try to "square" the theology of Jesus with "later Christian dogma" *(Historical Figure,* 2). Those Christians who envision Jesus as an eschatological prophet must come to grips with the fact that Jesus in one critical aspect was wrong: The kingdom did not come.[18] Sanders provides only a partial answer: "He went to his death. His followers, by carrying through the logic of his own position in a transformed situation, created a movement which would grow and continue to alter in ways unforeseeable in Jesus' own time, but in progressive steps, each one explicable in its own historical context" *(Jesus and Judaism,* 340).

Jesus the Millenarian Prophet

Other scholars have taken up the mantle of reconstructing Jesus as an eschatological prophet. Dale Allison, for example, forcefully presents Jesus as a millenarian ascetic. Allison agrees that Jesus proclaimed the restoration of Israel, but he differs significantly from Sanders by arguing that (a) Jesus rejected covenantal nomism and (b) called for repentance.[19] Allison also pushes the eschatological debate forward with his discussion of the Jesus movement within the larger category of millenarian movements.

Allison's doctoral dissertation argued that Jesus associated himself with the Son of man in Daniel 7, and, therefore, Jesus and his followers expected an imminent parousia initiated by a final tribulation.[20] Jesus predicted that he and they might die in the tribulation, but he also predicted his resurrection and saw it as the onset of the general resurrection of the dead (80). Jesus' death and resurrection were later interpreted as the inauguration of a longer process of eschatological fulfillment. So Allison suggests a greater continuity between the predictions of Jesus and the teachings of the church, a harmony that "nourished the belief that eschatological promises had begun to be fulfilled" (149).

In a later article, Allison critiques both "conservative" scholars who refuse to acknowledge the "humiliating discovery" that Jesus proclaimed the imminent end of the world and "more radical" scholars who produce an "aphoristic sage."[21] Allison has to admit that Jesus, like all millenarian prophets, was wrong about the imminent end of the world (218). At this point, though, Allison has no real theological answer about the relevancy—or adequacy—of a mistaken eschatological Jesus. Only later will he examine how an apocalyptic prophet can be relevant for Christian faith.[22]

Jesus of Nazareth

Allison believes that a scholar should begin with a "paradigm," an explanatory matrix by which to order the data about Jesus (36). This paradigm should be in place "prior to and independently of our evaluation of the historicity of individual items in the Jesus tradition" (39). This approach sounds similar to the accusation leveled against the Jesus Seminar that they arrived at a predetermined portrait of Jesus. The positive aspect is that Allison openly presents his interpretive frame of reference, which allows others to critique those presuppositions.

Allison chooses the hypothesis of an eschatological Jesus because of that theory's simplicity, scope, explanatory power, and parallels in the history of religion. For example, passages from a wide variety of sources indicate that John the Baptist, with whom Jesus was associated, and many early followers of Jesus thought that the eschatological climax was imminent. This continuity of thought makes it likely that Jesus did as well. Likewise, the entire Hellenistic-Roman world was dominated by "prophetic eschatology," and the apocalyptic writings of

Judaism share this eschatological spirit. Social and political circumstances were ripe for a millenarian movement with a sense of an imminent transformation, and Jesus and some of his contemporaries shared eschatological hopes for Jewish restoration (39–44).

Allison contends that many sayings from the gospels—such as the coming of the Son of man, the eschatological judgment, and Jesus' presupposition that the final fulfillment of God's saving work is imminent—fit within that eschatological framework (44). Many of the major themes of Jesus' teaching readily invite if not demand an eschatological interpretation. Furthermore, we can discern Jesus' congruence with the "standard pattern of Jewish messianism," as well as with millennial movements worldwide (48, 61–69, 78–94).[23]

Like Sanders, then, Allison sees Jesus as a Jewish prophet whose chief goal was the eschatological restoration of Israel (69). Allison moves beyond Sanders, though, by claiming that Jesus was the leader of a millenarian movement, and he compares the Jesus movement with millenarian movements in other places and eras.

Allison also reminds us—as C. J. Cadoux and others had noted—that such passages as the woes upon the cities in Galilee (e.g., Luke 10:13–15) reflect Jesus' "real and passionate disappointment" in at least some of his expectations (150).[24] Like other millennial movements, Jesus and his followers found eschatological enthusiasm difficult to maintain over time: "Doubts come easily and rapidly" (150).

Allison also correctly states that Jesus' words of judgment and restoration were meant literally, not metaphorically, as G. B. Caird, N. T. Wright, and others have claimed. The imminent parousia of the Son of man (e.g., Mark 13:24–27) also cannot be deflected, as Wright attempts to do, by making it a symbolic prophecy of Jerusalem's destruction (160).

A Millenarian Ascetic

An integral part of Jesus' eschatological urgency, Allison argues, is that Jesus was a millenarian *ascetic*. That term is usually not associated with Jesus—who came "eating and drinking" (Luke 7:34)—but Allison seems to be reacting against Robert Funk's depiction of Jesus as "the proverbial party animal."[25] Allison's designation is extremely restricted, though: "In at least two respects the Jesus tradition clearly moves in ascetic directions" (174).

Jesus' attitude toward wealth demonstrates ascetic tendencies: Jesus asked "at least some individuals" to give away all they owned, and he himself abandoned family, work, and home (e.g., Luke 9:58). Jesus also actively practiced and promoted sexual asceticism. He praised life-long celibacy (Matt 19:10–12) and set a fence around the Torah by condemning lust, not just adultery (175–76). Allison argues that this type of asceticism is linked with eschatology. Just as altering the roles of men and women in the resurrected state (no more marriage; Mark 12:18–27) is a sign of the new order, Jesus' sexual continence was part and parcel of his eschatological expectation. The imminent arrival of the kingdom of God required "sacrificing a normal course of life" (201–2). In addition, the renunciation of families and possessions also indicates that Jesus wanted changes in this world to illustrate how things were to be different in the kingdom of God (210).

At this point Allison underestimates just how difficult a life Jesus and other peasant artisans must have led in first-century Palestine. Jesus did not "marginalize himself" (205) or choose to "live in poverty" (215); the powerful elite of the first century had marginalized the vast majority of the population. Jesus' alienation from the world stemmed at least in part from the oppression under which most people in Galilee suffered, and his statements about wealth are more a prophetic critique than asceticism.

Conclusion

Allison acknowledges that his work is a partial first step in making a complete case. The fact that he spends as much time critiquing "noneschatological Jesus" scholars as he does making the case for a "millenarian ascetic Jesus" certainly hampers his efforts to argue persuasively. Even his discussion about common features of millenarianism, which is critical for his arguments, is contained in a "Detached Note" (78–94), not a full chapter. Many gaps remain to be filled—especially about millenarianism—and a stronger, more sustained argument is needed. Allison, however, made a compelling start.

Jesus the King of the Jews[26]

Paula Fredriksen, like Sanders, attempts to start with "facts" as "fixed points" in her investigation (7). The most assured fact is Jesus' death on a Roman cross, a method of execution reserved for political insurrectionists. As Sanders had observed earlier, Fredriksen notes that if Rome thought Jesus was a real political threat, then at least some of Jesus' followers would have been executed. So Fredriksen begins with the question: Why was Jesus crucified?

Jesus was an exorcist and miracle-worker. His death on a cross, though, makes it "mysterious" as to why the earliest Christian tradition would choose the title *Messiah* for him, since the role of the Messiah was to defeat the enemies of God, reign over a restored Israel, and epitomize the military prowess of King David (124). But the fact that Jesus died on a Roman cross is our surest evidence that the claim of Davidic messiahship dates from his lifetime (137). Jesus either claimed it for himself or, as Fredriksen believes, others claimed it for him; in either case, it led directly to his death.

Fredriksen disagrees with Sanders that the temple action was a symbolic enacting of an apocalyptic prophecy about the imminent destruction of the temple (226). Jesus' overturning the tables of the moneychangers—if it happened—would have been witnessed only by a small fraction of the tens of thousands of people in the temple during Passover (232). That action, contrary to Sanders's contention, could not have led to Jesus' death.

Fredriksen believes that Jesus was executed because Jewish pilgrims hailed him as the Messiah during his triumphal entry into Jerusalem. Pilate killed him as a messianic pretender, not because *Jesus* thought he was the Messiah, but because *others* proclaimed that he was. Pilate crucified Jesus (and Jesus alone), but he knew that Jesus was not a political insurrectionist. How did Pilate know? Fredriksen argues that Pilate and the chief priests probably had plenty of information about Jesus, because Jesus, as portrayed in the Gospel of John, had taught openly in Jerusalem for years (241). But Jesus' triumphal entry into Jerusalem, with a crowd noisily proclaiming the coming of the kingdom of God, provoked Pilate's concern (242). Jesus himself did not claim to be the Messiah; his closest followers did not believe this; it sprang from those who did not know him well (247). "Perhaps" Jesus had announced that this Passover would be the last before the kingdom arrived, and this excited the apocalyptic expectations of the crowd (257).

Pilate and the chief priests were responsible for keeping the peace; they had to act. Jesus was arrested at night and crucified early in the morning so that Jerusalem would wake up with a "public service announcement" of what happens to those who claim to be King of the Jews (254). Without the enthusiastic crowd proclaiming (incorrectly) Jesus as the Messiah, Pilate would have had no reason to crucify him. The crowd's misplaced fervor led directly to Jesus' death (257).

Fredriksen thus claims that Jesus' death was a result of a (tragic) mistaken identity. Missing from her reconstruction, however, is the evidence that Sanders marshals to demonstrate that Jesus' self-claim was rather grandiose. Riding into Jerusalem on a donkey, for example, probably was a prophetic claim to be the "viceroy-to-be" of God.

Fredriksen's reconstruction thus is not as compelling as Sanders's. Her argument that the triumphal entry directly provoked Jesus' death cannot account for the delay between the entry into Jerusalem and his arrest. Likewise, her hypothesis assumes that the early Christians adopted the (erroneous) acclamation from an ignorant crowd about Jesus' messiahship—which they knew was incorrect—despite the fact that it was precisely this claim that led to his death.[27]

Like Sanders, Fredriksen ignores many of the parables and aphorisms of Jesus. Foxes have holes and birds of the air have nests, but many of Jesus' sayings have no home in this book. What is also missing—even more than in Sanders's reconstruction—is any real description of how Jesus was distinctive within Judaism. The traditions that portray Jesus as engaging in controversies with opponents are downplayed or seen as later creations. This results in a more flattering portrayal of Jesus' opponents—a corrective to the negative stereotypes in some scholarship—but the pendulum seems to have swung too far. Finally, based on what (little) we know of Pilate, Sanders's position may be closer to the truth: Pilate without a second thought, on the high priest's recommendation, ordered Jesus' execution. Fredriksen's reconstruction leaves many questions unanswered.

Conclusion

Jesus most likely expected an imminent inbreaking of the kingdom of God, and he spoke of it literally, not metaphorically. Sanders's portrait of Jesus, though, relates only part of the story, because he downplays the social and economic implications of Jesus' message. Allison's reconstruction refines this portrait in several ways: First, he situates the Jesus movement within the larger context of millennial movements. Second, he does not minimize the conflicts between Jesus and his contemporaries. Third, Allison correctly realizes that although much of Jesus' teaching

was eschatological, not everything was. Jesus' ethical imperatives, for example, cannot be reduced to eschatology. Neither can
many of the themes of his public activity, including his depiction
of God as a caring father, his emphasis on the love, compassion,
and forgiveness of God, and God's "special regard for the unfortunate." This acknowledgement has also led Allison to begin to
address the social and economic elements of Jesus' message,
although much more is needed to reach a more complete portrait.

Millenarian movements such as the one Jesus began not
only anticipate how things will work in the future; they often
demand changes in the present. As John Kloppenborg aptly
observed, apocalyptic eschatology has the potential as a destabilizing, threatening, and subversive force that can serve to demand
alternative social practices in the present.[28] In addition, Bruce
Malina argues that peasant societies such as first-century Galilee
did not have a tension between the "now" and the "not yet." What
we see as "future-oriented" sayings would have been interpreted
as "present-oriented" by first-century peasants.[29]

Reconstructions of the historical Jesus must come to terms
with Jesus in his first-century context as both an apocalyptic
prophet and a champion of social and economic justice for an
oppressed people. Any portrait that does not address both these
aspects provides only a partial and somewhat slanted glimpse of
Jesus of Nazareth.

5

The Mediterranean Jewish Peasant and the Brokerless Kingdom

> "My pastor told me not to come here tonight because you are even to the left of Borg."
>
> "Give your pastor my best regards," [Crossan] replied, "and tell him that is the good news. The bad news is that both Borg and Crossan are to the right of Jesus. And worse still, if he will recall Psalm 110, Jesus is to the right of God."[1]

For more than three decades, John Dominic Crossan has produced major contributions to the study of the historical Jesus. The best way to understand Crossan's prolific scholarly odyssey is to trace the development of his thought in his numerous books on the parables, Jesus, and early Christianity.

A Long Way from Tipperary

In contrast to many scholars, Crossan reflects on how his life experiences affect his view of the historical Jesus. For example, in Crossan's autobiography, *A Long Way from Tipperary,* he wonders whether it was Joseph's absence that led Jesus to emphasize God as Father. Crossan would never speak of God in that way, because

Crossan's "earthly father was all [he] could ever wish for in a father..." (39). Likewise, how much did Crossan's study of Irish history—especially the years of British rule—influence his conception of systemic evil and its condemnation in the teachings of Jesus? Is that what leads Crossan to ask whether the burning of Sepphoris and the enslaving of its inhabitants by the Romans during the Jewish revolt in 4 BCE affected Mary and her young son Jesus? What happened to the small village of Nazareth, just three and a half miles to the southeast of Sepphoris (50)? What would Mary have told Jesus of this destruction? Did it affect his view of power, oppression, and Roman rule? Crossan believes that Mary's character—and, in turn, Jesus'—was formed not just by the general Jewish hope for God's justice, but also by the specific experience of the Roman army's slaughtering of people in Galilee (52).

Crossan was influenced by his nineteen years as a Servite monk and priest (28). He was impressed, for example, by elements of equality among the Servites: Everyone dressed the same and ate the same food, from the Father prior to the youngest novice. His novitiate was exhilarating; he "loved it wholeheartedly and passionately" (58). He earned a doctorate in biblical studies and did postdoctoral work at the Pontifical Biblical Institute in Rome and at the École Biblique in Jerusalem. By the 1960's, the monastic priesthood had become less important to him than biblical studies, and celibacy had become less important than female companionship. Crossan left monastery and priesthood, however, not because he refused future celibacy, but because he refused future obedience (80): "Not even a vow of obedience could make me sing a song I did not hear" (86). As an ex-priest and monk, it was difficult finding a teaching position, but DePaul University in Chicago offered him an associate professorship in 1969. He stayed at DePaul for the rest of his career (95).

The word *parable* is constitutive for all of Crossan's work on the historical Jesus and earliest Christianity (112). When Jesus wanted to say something important about God, he did so via parable; when the early church wanted to say something important about Jesus, they too went into parable: "the parabler had become parabled" (168).[2] For example, the nature miracles in the gospels "scream parable" at Crossan; not history, not miracle, but parable (167). Even the feeding of the 4000/5000 is a miracle-in-parable that commands the disciples—and the church—to make sure that food is distributed fairly and equitably to all (168).

The Parables of Jesus

Crossan's *In Parables: The Challenge of the Historical Jesus* examined the historical Jesus not in the sense of his religion, faith, or self-understanding, but in the sense of Jesus' language.[3] The parables of Jesus, for Crossan, reflect the temporality of Jesus' experience of God, establish the historicity of his response to God's kingdom, and they "create and establish the historical situation of Jesus himself" (32).

These poetic metaphors, Crossan asserts, portray a "permanent eschatology," the continuous presence of the God who challenges the world and repeatedly shatters its complacency. The kingdom of God and its parables manifest an *advent* of a radical new world of possibility, a *reversal* of expectations, and a call to *action* as an expression of the new world with new possibilities (26–27).[4]

In Fragments: The Aphorisms of Jesus

In Fragments represents significant turning points in Crossan's scholarly and personal journeys. On a personal level, Crossan completed working on the page proofs shortly after his wife Margaret died.[5] On a scholarly level, his focus on the historical Jesus now turned from the parabolic tradition to the aphoristic tradition.

Crossan focused on the 133 aphorisms found in Mark and Q, including dependent versions in Matthew and Luke, and independent versions elsewhere—both in canonical and noncanonical sources. He identified, organized, and analyzed the stages of development of these 133 sayings. Since these sayings were first spoken, not written, Crossan recognized that Jesus' sayings would have been heard as a verbal structure that could take many permutations: A *performancial* variation retains the verbal structure but in differing forms that still are "syntactically complete" (through contraction, expansion, conversion, substitution, or transposition). A *hermeneutical* variation gives an interpretation of the saying. After detailed analyses of aphoristic sayings, compounds, clusters, conclusions, dialogues, and stories, Crossan offered a diagram of how the aphoristic tradition could generate all of these various permutations (314–15).

This dense—in the best sense of the word—book is a model of methodological rigor. Crossan suggested innovative answers to a variety of questions concerning the processes of transmission and transformation, as well as how aphorisms could be categorized to illuminate each other.

Fundamental questions remain, however. Vernon K. Robbins's review of *In Fragments* correctly argued that the best term for these sayings is not *aphorism;* it is *chreia*—a concise statement or action attributed with aptness to some specific person or something analogous to a person.[6] A *chreia* could be a saying and/or action, and it speaks from within the horizons of a specific person's thought and action. Therefore, a *chreia* must not be isolated from the person to whom it is attributed, and, as Robbins notes, *within the rhetoric of the saying itself* are significant clues as to how Jesus applied the saying. Any attempt to reconstruct the teaching of Jesus must investigate the network of presuppositions inherent in the action and speech attributed to Jesus—a crucial aspect that Crossan overlooked.[7]

Four Other Gospels: Shadows on the Contours of Canon[8]

Crossan's *Four Other Gospels* is a preliminary attempt to write a literary history of the gospels that considered the traditions about Jesus in all gospel materials, not just the canonical gospels (183). His conclusions about the relationship between canonical and extracanonical gospels form the foundations for the decisions he makes in his later books about the historical Jesus.[9]

Crossan believes, for example, that the Gospel of Thomas is independent of the canonical gospels because there are no traces of common order between Thomas and the others, and the great majority of sayings in Thomas give no evidence of Thomas's dependence on the others (35–36).

Crossan offers a case study of the parable of the Great Supper (Matt 22:1–14; Luke 14:16–24; and Gospel of Thomas 64). He argues that Luke and especially Matthew have retrojected allegorical descriptions of early Christianity's relationship to Judaism into their versions (50). The Gospel of Thomas adds an interpretation to the parable—about businessmen and merchants not entering the places of the Father—but its response is closer to Jesus' parable than are Luke's and Matthew's versions.

Crossan's more controversial conclusion about the Gospel of Peter is that it contains three units—what he calls the Passion-Resurrection Source but later named the "Cross Gospel"—that are independent of the four canonical gospels and that served as a source for all four canonical gospels (Gospel of Peter 1:1–6:22; 7:25–9:34; 9:35–11:49). The Gospel of Peter also contains three units, however, that are dependent on the canonical gospels. Crossan offers a "working hypothesis" that Gospel of Peter 1:1–6:22 was the first stage of the passion narrative. The second stage was Mark's redaction of that source. The third stage was that of Matthew and Luke, each of which had the passion narratives of Peter and Mark. The Gospel of John then utilized the synoptic gospels and Peter, and it incorporated elements of Peter that were omitted by Mark (e.g., the unbroken legs; 145–46). Finally, under pressure to adapt itself to the (later) canonical gospels—including the stories of the empty tomb—the Gospel of Peter was written as an expansion of the earlier Passion-Resurrection Source.[10]

Crossan's meticulous work is often brilliantly argued but is also ultimately unconvincing. Most scholars rightly conclude that the Gospel of Thomas and the Gospel of Peter are both dependent upon canonical gospels. Crossan's hypotheses remain minority opinions.

The Cross That Spoke[11]

On the hundredth anniversary of the discovery of the Gospel of Peter, Crossan revisited his proposal that three sections of the Gospel of Peter—what he now labels the "Cross Gospel"—served as the source for the passion narrative in Mark, and, along with Mark, for the other canonical gospels.[12]

I remain unconvinced that a Cross Gospel served as a source for all four canonical gospels. Crossan does not completely answer Dennis MacDonald's objection that if Matthew, Luke, and John all used the Cross Gospel and Mark, then one would expect some cases in which two of them would prefer the Cross Gospel to Mark rather than using Mark consistently.[13] It seems more likely, however, that sections of the Gospel of Peter are elaborations of earlier traditions. The resurrection account, for example, seems to follow the trajectory of providing more eyewitness evidence of the resurrection as the tradition develops (e.g., the Roman soldiers and Jewish authorities; Gospel of Peter 8:31–10:42). In addition, the centurion receives a name (Petronius) in the Gospel of Peter, which conforms to the tendency of later apocryphal gospels to provide names for characters who are anonymous earlier in the tradition.[14]

Other objections can be raised about Crossan's reconstruction. John's passion narrative probably is independent of the synoptic passion narratives, although there are indications of linkages through oral traditions (e.g., Mark 14:54, 67; John 18:18, 25). In addition, since almost all of the Gospel of Peter is found in a single late manuscript, copyists of its text could have incorporated aspects of Matthew, Mark, Luke, and John into the Gospel of Peter.[15] Although some sections of the Gospel of Peter may indeed reflect early traditions, when considering the diverse passion and resurrection stories contained in the four canonical gospels, dependence on a "Cross Gospel" is exceedingly unlikely.

The Historical Jesus[16]

Crossan's *The Historical Jesus* assured his status as a premier historical Jesus scholar. The first three pages of the work (xi–xiii) not only encapsulate Crossan's overall conclusions about Jesus, but they are the most eloquent words written about Jesus since Albert Schweitzer's conclusion in *The Quest of the Historical Jesus*.

Methodology: Sources, Stratification, and Attestation

Crossan calls the "stunning diversity" of reconstructions of the historical Jesus "an academic embarrassment" (xxviii), and these discordant portraits force Crossan back to methodology. He argues that without "scientific stratigraphy"—a "detailed location of every item in its proper chronological layer"—scholars can reach almost any conclusion. Therefore, Crossan proposes a method and tries to follow it "stringently" (xxviii).

His approach includes a complex triple, triadic process. The first triad involves the reciprocal interplay of social *anthropology,* Hellenistic-Roman *history,* and the *literature* of the specific sayings and stories from and about Jesus.

Crossan highlights what many New Testament scholars ignore, obscure, or deny: The problem of reconstructing the historical Jesus stems directly from the nature of the sources. If you

compare the canonical gospels side-by-side, for example, disagreement rather than agreement jumps out at you. More importantly, the discrepancies between accounts are not only due to the
vagaries of memory or divergences in emphasis; they stem from
deliberate theological (re)interpretations. In addition, the presence of the risen Jesus in the midst of the early Christian communities engendered a creative freedom, because Jesus was still
speaking through early Christian prophets. Thus the Jesus tradition involves at least three layers: retention, development, and
creation of new sayings and stories (xxx–xxxi).

To tackle this problem, Crossan's second triad digs through
the "sedimented layers to find what Jesus actually said and did."
The first step is to *inventory* all of the major sources, placing them
into their historical contexts and literary relationships. The second step is to *stratify* the sources, positioning them in a chronological sequence within four strata: 30–60 CE, 60–80 CE, 80–120
CE, and 120–150 CE. Third, Crossan examines whether a unit
appears in multiple, independent sources (xxxi).

Crossan's third triad manipulates the data: The first step
stresses the *sequence of strata*. Even though a unit from the fourth
stratum (120–150 CE) may be more original than one from the first
stratum (30–60 CE), Crossan decides that scholarly integrity
demands that he work almost exclusively with the first stratum.
Crossan inventories and stratifies all units in an appendix (427–50),
which includes his decision whether the tradition was originally
from Jesus (+) or not (–). The second step establishes a *hierarchy of
attestation*. In other words, he begins with the first stratum but
focuses on the units and complexes that have the highest number of
independent attestations. So, in Crossan's view, the lower the stratum level and the higher the number of independent attestations,
the greater the probability that the unit of Jesus tradition gives us
solid historical data. The final element is a *bracketing of singular-
ity*. If a unit is mentioned only once (independently) in the
sources—even in the first stratum—Crossan avoids using that unit
in his reconstruction (xxxii–xxxiii).

The Brokered, Broken Empire

The section on "Brokered Empire" (1–88) discusses the anthropological, economic, and historical contexts in the first-century Mediterranean world, including such "universals" as honor/shame and patron-client relations. Crossan also includes some archaeological data in his analysis (15–16) and extensively explores what life would be like for a peasant artisan in the first century (e.g., 29).

The second section, "Embattled Brokerage" (89–224), delineates Crossan's views of the effects of Roman imperialism on Jewish peasantry and the various reactions against that imperialism. The Jewish peasantry of first-century Palestine was pushed below a bare subsistence level of existence and into a relative, perceived, and decremental deprivation, resulting eventually in the massive peasant rebellion of 66–73 CE (221). A major aspect of this economic decline involved small independent farmers, artisans, and the urban poor of Jerusalem who fell heavily into debt. Many small farmers, for example, were pushed into tenancy, day-laboring, and even slavery (222). Such oppression provoked various reactions from those within society who felt systematically excluded: passive resistance, nonviolent resistance (e.g., an agrarian strike; 128–36), witchcraft/magic, millenarianism or apocalypticism, social banditry, and, finally, political revolution.

A Brokerless Kingdom

Crossan argues that Jesus proclaimed a "brokerless kingdom" in response to this oppression (225–426). The earliest stages of the Jesus tradition indicate that Jesus was understood both as a sapiential (wisdom) teacher and as an apocalyptic prophet (230). Crossan sees this as evidence that Jesus initially believed in John the Baptist's apocalyptic message, but that he changed his mind after John's execution (237, 259). For Crossan, Luke 7:24–28 (the least in the kingdom is greater than John) is further evidence that Jesus came to repudiate John's apocalyptic vision. Crossan argues on the basis of this tenuous evidence that Jesus changed from an apocalyptic viewpoint to a sapiential one.

Not all of Crossan's eggs are in one basket, however. He supports Kloppenborg's stratification of Q into different layers, with the earliest layer being primarily sapiential.[17] He argues that the apocalyptic Son of man sayings are not from Jesus (they stem from early Christian reflection on Daniel 7:13), even though Jesus' apocalyptic "coming on the clouds" saying in Matthew 24:29, 30b–31 (Luke 21:25–28) is from the first stratum and attested six times. Other apocalyptic sayings from the first stratum and attested multiple times are judged to be inauthentic as well (e.g. the "before the angels" saying of Mark 8:38/Matt 16:27/Luke 9:26 is from the first stratum and is attested four times). In these instances, Crossan departs from his "stringent" methodology in order to preserve a nonapocalyptic Jesus.

Jesus, Crossan believes, lived in a system of open commensality, an egalitarian sharing of spiritual and material resources (341) that served as Jesus' strategy for rebuilding peasant community (262, 344). It is a present, sapiential kingdom of "nobodies" (269) and the "destitute"—the unclean, degraded, and expendable (273). Jesus, as an exorcist and a healer, offered an alternative means to God rather than those sanctioned by the dominant religious institution (309), and his healings demonstrated what God's kingdom looked like (332). Even Jesus' itinerancy is a symbolic representation of "unbrokered" egalitarianism; Jesus and his followers refuse to settle down in one place and establish a "brokered" (patron-broker-client) presence (346).

The temple episode's "symbolic destruction" is a logical extension of Jesus' radical social egalitarianism (357–61).[18] Yet, for Crossan, most of the passion narrative is "prophecy historicized": creations of the gospel authors based primarily on their readings of the Hebrew Bible and their expressions of faith and hope (372). Mark, for example, created the story of Jesus' burial. Roman soldiers normally stayed with victims of crucifixion until their death and then buried the bodies themselves (392). In reality, Crossan says, nobody knew what happened to Jesus' body. At best, his followers hoped his body was buried (394).

Crossan concludes that Jesus must be understood within "his contemporary Judaism" but correctly notes that early-first-century Judaism was "a richly creative, diverse, and variegated one" (417). His reconstruction suggests that Jesus was a rural peasant Jewish Cynic. Jesus' strategy involved free healing and common eating, a religious and economic egalitarianism that was calculated to force individuals into "unmediated physical and spiritual contact with God and with each other"—the brokerless kingdom of God (421–22).

Reactions and Critiques

Crossan attempts to take seriously the cultural contexts of the first-century Mediterranean world. Yet significant problems arise with how he uses these data. John Elliott, for example, notes that the theory that Jesus promoted "egalitarianism" is fatally flawed, because egalitarianism was a product of the Enlightenment. In reality, the household/family—organized on stratified, not egalitarian, lines—was Jesus' chief metaphor for clarifying divine-human relationships and illustrating the nature and values of the kingdom of God.[19] Although Elliott wishes "with every fiber of [his] egalitarian being" that the Jesus movement had been egalitarian, he concludes that the theory "lacks probative textual and historical support, is sociologically implausible, conceptually anachronistic, and appears ideologically driven."[20]

Crossan's reconstruction of the historical Jesus stands or falls on some questionable foundations (cf. xxxiv)—the proverbial house built on sand that is first stratum but only singly-attested (Matt 7:24–27/Luke 6:47–49). Few scholars agree with Crossan's inclusion of the Gospel of Thomas, the Egerton Gospel, the Gospel of the Hebrews, and the Cross Gospel in the earliest stratum (30–60 CE). This questionable stratification increases the problematic nature of Crossan's dependence on the criterion of multiple attestation with his first stratum sources. In addition, any methodology that excludes such data as the (singly attested) parable of the Good Samaritan or the Prodigal Son leaves something to be desired. This approach produces as idiosyncratic a picture of Jesus as does an overdependence on the criterion of dissimilarity. Crossan's methodology is rigorous and gives the appearance of some objectivity, but it seems limited, antiseptic, and mechanical—as well as ultimately unsatisfying.

Jesus: A Revolutionary Biography[21]

Crossan wryly notes in his autobiography that his massive *The Historical Jesus* was for his scholarly peers and was "never intended for normal human consumption." He confesses that he "noted exactly where and when [his] wife's bookmark stopped moving," so he wrote the 209-page *Jesus: A Revolutionary Biography* as an "apology" for all those who started the larger book but did not finish it.[22] Crossan also promises that every chapter contains "something beyond the parent volume" (xiv).

Crossan tries to envision how Jesus' present, sapiential kingdom of God would look to peasants (58). It was a kingdom of "nobodies," one which involved an attack on first-century families and family values, one which practiced "open commensality" in which anyone could be reclining next to anyone else at the shared table—female and male, free and slave, artisan and retainer, and ritually pure and impure (68). Jesus used the meal to signify unity, symbolize that God was present in the meal, and proclaim that everyone should have equal shares of both God and food.

Jesus' radical vision and actions—such as his breaking of purity rules by touching/healing a leper—put him on a direct collision course with the priestly authorities (83).[23] Jesus was a Mediterranean Jewish peasant, one whose teachings and actions most closely resemble Cynicism (e.g., Luke 10:4), even if Jesus knew nothing about Cynicism (106–22). Both are populists who appeal to ordinary people, and whose lifestyles match their words about such things as worldly possessions. Yet Cynics are urban; Jesus is rural. Jesus organized a communal movement; Cynics are more individualistic. As Crossan muses: "Maybe Jesus is what peasant *Jewish* Cynicism looks like" (122).

The chapter "The Dogs Beneath the Cross" blaringly proclaims Crossan's changed perspective about what happened to Jesus' body after the crucifixion. Crossan now declares that wild beasts probably ate Jesus' corpse: His body was either left on the cross and devoured by carrion crows and scavenger dogs (127) or buried by Roman soldiers in a shallow grave only to be dug up and eaten by wild dogs (154). When asked about that "offensive" hypothesis, Crossan noted the probable impact upon his readers: "For the first time, maybe in their whole lives, they get a whiff of what it was like to know Jesus, to be on Jesus' side, and to know he was crucified."[24] Crossan argues that it is impossible for us to imagine the offhanded brutality, anonymity, and indifference with which a peasant like Jesus would have been executed—the pain, horror, and humiliation (196).

Crossan also believes that the resurrection accounts tell us nothing about the origins of Christian faith but quite a lot about the origins of Christian authority—power and leadership in the earliest Christian communities (e.g., Peter and the Beloved Disciple in John 20:3–10 or the denigration of Mary Magdalene's authority in John 20:1–2, 11–18). All we know is that those who had experienced Jesus' divine power during his lifetime continued to do so after his death in ways not confined by time or place (197).

Who Killed Jesus?[25]

In this book, Crossan reexamines the passion narratives and conducts a running debate with Raymond Brown's *The Death of the Messiah*.[26] Crossan returns to his theme that the passion and resurrection narratives are primarily prophecy historicized—created assertions that Jesus fulfilled some prophecy. For example, the darkness at noon during Jesus' execution is not historical; it is based on early Christian reflection on such passages as Amos 8:9–10, where darkness at noon symbolizes a terrible catastrophe (3). Crossan's working hypothesis is that specific units, general sequences, and even the overall framework of the passion/resurrection accounts were subject to similar processes (4). This distinction between history remembered and prophecy historicized is especially important in the passion narratives, because those narratives unfortunately "have been the seedbed for Christian anti-Judaism," as well as anti-Semitism, with horrifying results (35–36).[27]

Crossan imagines that "learned followers" of Jesus searched the scriptures to understand his fate and destiny. They looked for texts such as Psalm 2, with a dialectic of persecution and vindication. In addition, since Jesus probably was flogged as part of the regular brutality preparatory to Roman crucifixion, other elements of the narrative were created by using the popular scapegoat ritual, the "mocked king theater," and reflection on such scriptures as Isaiah 50:6, Zechariah 12:10, and Zechariah 3:1–5 (132).

Crossan once again argues that Jesus' burial and the empty tomb are not historical. Neither are the "risen apparitions" historical in the sense of trances or ecstasies—with the exception of Paul's vision. After the death of Jesus, however, some of Jesus' followers found that the empowering kingdom was still present and operative in history. Trances and ecstasies were creative ways of expressing that faith, and risen appearances were dramatic ways of organizing and managing that faith. But Christian faith itself was the experience of the continued empowering presence of absolutely the same Jesus in an absolutely different mode of existence (209–10).

This book demonstrates that early Christian reflection on the Hebrew Bible produced developments in the passion narratives—but that is hardly news to scholars. The disagreement is over the *extent* of those developments, and Crossan leans heavily to the side of creation. It appears, however, that Crossan has "searched" the

Hebrew Bible prophecies even more extensively and more creatively than did the first-century "learned followers" of Jesus.

The Birth of Christianity

Crossan declares that this book is the closest possible sequel to *The Historical Jesus* (17), because it examines the "lost years of earliest Christianity" (30–50 CE). *The Historical Jesus* focused on the "conception" of Christianity—Jesus' kingdom-of-God movement in the 20's CE. The "birth" of Christianity or Christian Judaism—the focus of this book—was that movement's continuation as Jesus' companions wrestled to imitate his life and understand his death (x).

Continuation and Reconstruction

Initial sections of the book reprise Crossan's reconstruction of the historical Jesus and include responses to critics of that reconstruction. He also argues that scholars must not "quarantine" elements of Jesus' life from historical judgments. If we make judgments about the divine conception of Alexander, Augustus, Buddha, or other historical figures, for example, we are ethically committed to doing the same for Jesus of Nazareth. Even though we can never know the "real" Jesus any more than we could ever know the reality of any human being, this uncertainty does not preclude the ethical necessity of such judgments (31). Crossan's *sarcophilic* position connects body and spirit: The historical Jesus and the risen Jesus are one and the same (39), but the risen Jesus should still carry the wounds of crucifixion. Those wounds are the marks of history; to understand Jesus' death, you need to know about his life (40).[28]

Crossan's arguments here are compelling. Every generation must reconstruct the historical Jesus as best they can at any time and place (45). Our *best* theories and methods are just that: *our* (limited, dated, and doomed) theories and methods, but that dialogic process involving voices both past and present is not just possible; it is absolutely necessary.

Memory and Orality

Crossan reexamines how the Jesus materials were transmitted in the forty years between the death of Jesus and the writing of Mark's Gospel. He criticizes the sanguine acceptance of scholars such as N. T. Wright of a "controlled oral tradition," where the "sayings remain more or less identical" (49). The myth of a controlled oral tradition assumes that there is a fixed (scribal) text— something that did not exist until after the first gospel was written (51). Although the *structure* persists in memory, the *elements* can be freely organized in oral performance.[29]

Methodology and Anthropology

Crossan again focuses on methodology, because scholars' long-utilized criteria have not led to any consensus. Criteria, no matter how good, do not constitute a method unless they are theoretically organized into an operational system (144–45). In this book, Crossan refines his interdisciplinary method. He begins with context and uses cross-cultural anthropology, Judeo-Roman history, and archaeology to present the sharpest possible reconstruction of life in Lower Galilee. Second, Crossan again stratifies the texts into layers and works primarily with what he considers the earliest layer. Finally, he looks for close conjunctions between the sharpest image of context and the earliest layer of text, because that gives the best historical reconstruction of Jesus and his companions presently available (149).

Is Crossan's approach an improvement over other scholars' approaches? His methodology relies on his idiosyncratic view of the sources, but it also often depends on his vision of plausibility. In fact, *plausibility* sometimes trumps methodology, such as

Crossan's refusal to consider multiply attested apocalyptic sayings from his first stratum as authentic.

History and Archaeology

Crossan increasingly turns to archaeology to demonstrate that Lower Galilee was becoming more commercialized under Herod Antipas. His hypothesis, based on cross-cultural anthropology, is that peasant resistance increased because of this commercialization. Both Sepphoris and Tiberias—cities that Herod Antipas (re)built within twenty years and twenty miles of each other—created large populations (as much as 24,000 each) that realigned and stretched agricultural practices. No longer did Galilee consist of numerous self-sufficient farms or hamlets; the agricultural focus turned to feeding Sepphoris and Tiberias (221). The Jesus faction thus emerged as a kingdom-of-God movement of peasant resistance in response to Antipas's urbanization that seriously damaged peasant life (233, 235).

Kingdom and Eschatology

Although, in Crossan's estimation, Q and Thomas are independent voices, the parallel content between them is exceptionally high (247). Crossan labels these parallel units the *Common Sayings Tradition,* and he works primarily with the 37 units in that common tradition. He explores these 37 sapiential units, because he believes they are the earliest traditions in Q and Thomas (255).

Crossan labels this early tradition "eschatological," because its vision was radical, countercultural, and this-world-negating. There are different types of eschatology, however. *Apocalyptic eschatology,* for example, negates the world by announcing that in the (usually imminent) future God will act to restore justice in this unjust world. *Ascetical eschatology,* on the other hand, negates the world by withdrawing from normal human life in terms of food, sex, speech, or occupation. *Ethical eschatology,* however, such as this

Common Sayings Tradition, negates the world by actively protesting and nonviolently resisting a system judged to be evil, unjust, and violent (282–87).

Healers and Itinerants

The Common Sayings Tradition demonstrates to Crossan that Jesus proclaimed an *ethical eschatology* and a present kingdom, in contrast to John the Baptist's apocalyptic eschatology. Jesus' program of healing is "bodily resistance"—nonviolent resistance that places God on the side of those injured by exploitation, malnutrition, and disease (293–304). God is "for" the destitute and powerless, because their situation is structurally unjust. Jesus speaks especially to recently dispossessed peasants seeking to restore their dignity and security in the name of God, those persons who have been struck hardest by Antipas's commercialization and urbanization, those who have moved from poverty to destitution. To those people whose families had failed under these pressures, Jesus offers an alternative family: the companionship of the kingdom of God (324–25).

Jesus, a *tekton* (peasant artisan; Mark 6:3), was a marginalized peasant trying to survive as a rural artisan or landless laborer (350–52). His voice cried out "from below," and his program united the destitute landless (itinerants) and the poor landed ones (householders) to rebuild the peasant community ripped apart by commercialization and urbanization. Itinerants eat with those who receive them and heal the sick in response. The kingdom of God was present in these interactions of itinerants and householders, in a new community of healing and eating, of shared material and spiritual resources (353).[30]

Conclusion

Crossan then focuses on what happened to the early Jesus traditions: The "Life Tradition" (how Jesus lived) predominated among the hamlets of Galilee and Syria. The "Death Tradition" (which emphasized Jesus' death and resurrection) is associated primarily with Jerusalem. Its earliest accessible form is the Cross Gospel, which was created in Jerusalem in the early 40's (527) and which incorporated the female lament tradition and the male exegetical tradition (572–73).

This book refines Crossan's earlier positions, so much of the same praise and criticism apply. Once again, Crossan's reconstruction is like a house of cards resting on his source analyses and built with his methodological approaches and interpretive decisions. Yet, unlike some scholars, Crossan's cards are mostly displayed on the table.

His task—to describe Jesus' vision and program and to reconstruct life in the earliest Christian communities—is extremely speculative. Yet the cumulative effect of the narrative voice in this book, with its authoritative pronouncements and engaging style, engenders an aura of definitive answers. This is not a criticism; rather it is an observation of Crossan's abilities as an author and scholar. But we need to step back, take a careful look, and evaluate just how tentative his reconstructions are.

Crossan's Jesus proclaims the Jewish God of justice. That reconstruction of Jesus, to me, is more attractive than most reconstructions. I want Jesus to rail against the injustices of the powers-that-be and to proclaim the radical new community in the kingdom of God. Such are my own predispositions. Yet this also reflects, in part, the message in many parables of Jesus, such as the condemnation of the unethical, wealthy elites in the Rich Man and Lazarus.[31]

Crossan captures a powerful aspect of the voice of Jesus the peasant artisan who condemned the exploitative, dominant class of his day. This same voice of Jesus provided hope to his fellow peasants and expendables that a compassionate and just God was on their side. As Crossan notes:

> Yahweh is a God not only of justice but also of compassion....But compassion, no matter how immediately necessary or profoundly human, cannot substitute for justice, for the *right* of all to equal dignity and integrity of life. Those who live by compassion are often canonized. Those who live by justice are often crucified (586).

Crossan is surely correct. Jesus of Nazareth lived with compassion and died because of his advocacy for justice. But that is only part of the story.

Excavating Jesus[32]

In this book, Crossan and Jonathan Reed combine archaeology and exegesis to "read stones and texts as an integrated whole" (xv–xvi). They begin with a list of what they consider the top ten archaeological discoveries[33] and the top ten exegetical discoveries[34] for "excavating Jesus." For example, in "How to Build a Kingdom" (51–97), they postulate two paradigmatic types of kingdoms. Jeroboam II's reign in the eighth century BCE—with a powerful monarch, splendid court, and luxurious aristocracy—is a prime example of a *commercial kingdom*. Amos's prophetic response to Jeroboam's reign represents a *covenantal kingdom:* He railed against the oppression of the poor by the rich, and he demanded not just individual righteousness, but also structural and systemic justice.

Commercial Kingdoms: Herod the Great and Herod Antipas

Crossan and Reed demonstrate that Herod the Great and Herod Antipas established commercial kingdoms within the greater commercial kingdom of the Roman Empire. Herod's famous building spree started with a series of opulent royal residences/fortresses. He next embarked on two immense projects—the city of Caesarea and the temple in Jerusalem. The magnificent city and modern harbor of Caesarea, named after the Emperor Augustus, established it as the eastern Mediterranean's busiest port. This magnificence, however, came with a price: Even with the income generated by the new harbor, the financial support for these building projects fell primarily to the peasants. To attempt to meet this increased financial burden, polycropping and self-sufficient family farms gave way to monocropping. Small landholders were more at risk, and many were forced into debt, lost their land, and became destitute.

On a smaller scale—as tetrarch not king, and in Galilee only—Herod Antipas followed in the footsteps of his father. He rebuilt Sepphoris into the "ornament of all Galilee" and as a miniature version of Caesarea. When Tiberius became emperor, Antipas built a new capital and named it Tiberias in his honor, just as his father named Caesarea after Augustus. Sepphoris and Tiberias, like Caesarea before them, were built with wealth generated from agricultural peasant labor, which placed a great strain on fields, vineyards, and olive trees. Once again, polycropping waned and monocropping increased, which left peasants perilously more threatened by crop failure or drought. Peasants increasingly could not pay their taxes or otherwise became indebted to buy necessities of life, both of which led eventually to the loss of their land. As architectural grandeur and wealth increased on one end of society, poverty and destitution increased on the other.

Covenantal Kingdom

Crossan and Reed stress that passages such as Leviticus 25:23 and Isaiah 5:8 demonstrate that the Jewish God is just, the land of Israel belongs to God, the land originally was distributed equitably, and God denounces the privileged few who unjustly dominate society. The Bible also forbids interest (Lev 25:35–37), remits indebtedness (Deut 15:1–2), liberates indebted slaves after seven years (Deut 15:12–14), and reverses dispossession (Lev 25:10). This is what a covenantal kingdom looks like.

Jesus' covenantal kingdom left behind no structures, inscriptions, or artifacts, but his proclamation likely was provoked by Herod Antipas's commercialization and urbanization. Crossan and Reed provide the "humble city of Capernaum" as evidence of the struggle and simplicity of life of the nonelite. There were no civic structures in Capernaum, no agora, and not even a public bathhouse or latrine. None of the streets were paved with stone or adorned with columns or porticoes. The houses, built with the local dark basalt, along with a few wood beams, straw or reeds, and mud, bespeak a simple existence of fishers and farmers. No luxury items or other indications of wealth have been found. Even the first-century fishing boat that was recently discovered indicates a struggling existence: This dilapidated 8-by-26-foot boat's construction, varied materials, and repairs speak of an experienced boatwright with sparse resources (85–86).

In this environment, Crossan and Reed argue, Jesus proclaimed an interdependent program of reciprocal sharing between destitute itinerants who provided spiritual gifts (healings) and the poor householders who provided material gifts (food). This commensality, constitutive of the kingdom of God and based on the ancient Jewish view of justice for the poor, seeks to restore the peasant society fractured by Antipas's urbanization and commercialization (126).

Conclusion

Crossan and Reed's collaborative efforts bear much fruit. Archaeological discoveries are not just visual aids or backdrops for the study of texts; the data provide insights that can challenge our assumptions about these texts and first-century society. Even if you disagree with their conclusions, Crossan and Reed illustrate that an interdisciplinary synthesis of archaeology, texts, and contexts illuminates the Jesus movement and Christian origins.

Conclusion: A Long Way Indeed from Tipperary

Crossan's numerous publications have brought him fame and notoriety. His rather eccentric source theories, dating and stratification of sources, and conclusions have proved controversial. With multiple attestation within the first stratum as the primary criterion (or the focus on the "Common Sayings Tradition" of Q and Thomas), Crossan's source theories become critically important. Using the criterion of multiple attestation primarily with the canonical gospels, for example, results in a much different portrait of Jesus. Crossan also leaves out many authentic sayings of Jesus because they are found in his second and third strata.[35] In addition, Crossan ignores multiply-attested apocalyptic elements in the first stratum as well as other multiply-attested items (e.g., Jesus' choosing of the Twelve) that fit within an apocalyptic viewpoint.

The vitriolic reactions against Crossan, however, have often been inaccurate and specious. Critics sometimes deride Crossan's "Cynic Jesus" as one that allegedly robs Jesus of his "Jewishness" and turns him into a "secular" figure. This criticism is, in William Arnal's words, a "manufactured controversy."[36] As Crossan notes, "I use the doctrine of Cynicism comparatively but do not need it constitutively. I have never considered a Cynic Jesus as some sort of replacement for a Jewish Jesus; indeed, I find that idea little short of absurd."[37]

First-century Judaism was diverse, and we should not retroject later norms of "orthodoxy" onto a more variegated earlier period. I differ with some of Arnal's conclusions, but he correctly observes that the rather shrill claims about the "Jewish Jesus" are usually associated with concerns to "protect" Jesus from Hellenistic influence (although all Judaism to a greater or lesser extent was influenced by Hellenism) and to "preserve" elements of a "traditional understanding" of Christianity. Crossan does not present a non-Jewish Jesus; in reality, the complaint is about the *nature* of his Jewishness (29).

Does Crossan overstress the social and economic elements of Jesus' message? Definitely. But, as Crossan observes, scholars such as Sanders ignore these elements at their peril: Ancient religion, economics, and politics were all inextricably intertwined.

Does Crossan reject significant data—sometimes even subverting his own methodology—that Jesus sometimes spoke in apocalyptic terms? Yes. Although Crossan affirms "ethical" eschatology, the evidence for the apocalyptic Jesus is significant, and it is even multiply attested within Crossan's first stratum. Crossan also relies on tenuous evidence to argue that Jesus initially believed in apocalyptic eschatology but changed his mind after the death of John the Baptist.

Apocalyptic and ethical eschatology are not as incongruent as Crossan seems to believe. As Dale Allison observes, an apocalyptic framework is just that, a framework, not the whole picture. Not all of the Jesus tradition is grounded in or generated by a belief in the imminent end of the world. Many people who believe in the imminent end of the world still actively promote a program for the present. Jesus' eschatological expectations added urgency to his message, but—as in other millennial movements that emphasize their indigenous heritage—most of his teachings drew from the deep well of Jewish tradition. Jesus looked forward, yes; but he also looked backward and engrossed himself in the will of God and how life in the kingdom should be lived—on earth and in heaven. This radical message is not just a dream about the future; it is a demand for the present.[38]

My reading of the Jesus traditions suggests that the resolution to this question thus is not *either* apocalyptic *or* ethical eschatology; it is some form of *both* apocalyptic *and* ethical eschatology. The future places immediate and significant demands upon the present. Crossan's portrait of Jesus, focusing primarily on present ethical eschatology, gives us a partial and relatively slanted glimpse of the historical Jesus.

6
The Elijah-like
Eschatological Prophet

> Whoever or whatever Jesus was, he was a complex figure,
> not easily subsumed under one theological rubric or socio-
> logical model. In this sense as well, he was a marginal Jew.
> In short, up to this point in our investigation the data suggest
> some sort of fusion of eschatological prophet, baptizer,
> exorcist, miracle-worker and healer, and rabbinic teacher of
> the law.[1]

On December 23, 1991, just in time for Christmas, the front
page of the *New York Times* included a story about the relationship between faith and historical Jesus research. Its author, Peter
Steinfels, profiled the recent books of two Roman Catholic aca-
demics, John Dominic Crossan and John P. Meier.[2] The books and
authors proved to be apt choices: Both Meier and Crossan were
ordained to the priesthood, earned degrees at the Pontifical Biblical Institute in Rome, taught at Catholic universities, and believed
that historical Jesus research was important. Yet Meier's more traditional perspective differs significantly from Crossan's more
radical approach.[3]

Meier originally planned a one-volume work on Jesus. That
vision expanded into two volumes and then into three (completed) volumes and a forthcoming fourth volume. The overall

series is entitled *A Marginal Jew: Rethinking the Historical Jesus,* and each volume is subtitled: Volume I, *The Roots of the Problem and the Person,* covers methodological issues and sketches Jesus' cultural context, familial background, and early years. Volume II, *Mentor, Message, and Miracles,* discusses John the Baptist and grapples with Jesus' message of the kingdom of God and the miracles attributed to him. Volume III, *Companions and Competitors,* examines the groups around Jesus and his direct and indirect "competitors." The fourth volume, *The Enigmas Jesus Posed and Was,* will treat four basic enigmas: Jesus' teaching on Jewish law, the parables, Jesus' self-designations, and Jesus' death.

Volume I: *The Roots of the Problem and the Person*[4]

Meier defines *historical Jesus* as "the Jesus whom we can recover, recapture, or reconstruct by using the scientific tools of modern historical research" (1). Meier envisions his task to be similar to his "fantasy of the 'unpapal conclave'" that would include a Catholic, a Protestant, a Jew, and an agnostic. These four persons—historians with appropriate knowledge of the first century CE—would be locked up in the bowels of Harvard Divinity School library, put on a spartan diet, and not be allowed to emerge until they had hammered out a consensus document on the identity, message, and life of Jesus of Nazareth.

Meier contends that the quest for the historical Jesus is important, because it gives greater "depth and color" to one's faith and reminds Christians that "faith in Christ" affirms one's adherence to a particular person who said and did particular things in a particular time and place in history. We should never lose sight of Jesus' humanity, and the quest helps to allay the domestication of Jesus by a "comfortable, respectable, bourgeois Christianity" and the co-opting of Jesus by political or other programs (196–200).

Meier chose the word *marginal* for his title because of the term's multiplicity of meaning: In non-Christian literature for a hundred years after his ministry, Jesus was at most a marginal "blip" on the radar screen. Jesus intentionally marginalized himself, by becoming "jobless and itinerant," by some of his practices and teachings, and by the fact that he was a "poor layman turned prophet and teacher" from rural Galilee (7–9). In addition, his trial and execution pushed him to the margins of society. Although some critics have taken the term *marginal* as his set definition for Jesus, Meier intended it to symbolize his refusal to give a set definition; it instead echoes the "riddle-speech of Jesus" (Volume II, 8).

Roots of the Problem

Meier accepts the majority view that Matthew and Luke independently used Mark and Q as sources. Thus we are left with three major independent sources: Mark, Q, and John (44). The rest of the New Testament yields limited data, and little can be gleaned from non-Christian sources such as Josephus and Tacitus. Meier also dismisses Crossan's Cross Gospel, as well as the view that the Gospel of Thomas is an independent source. In fact, Meier concludes that non-Christian and non-canonical materials give us no "reliable new information or authentic sayings that are independent of the [New Testament]" (140).

Meier collates five "primary criteria" and five "secondary" criteria to sift through the data:

The *criterion of embarrassment* focuses on actions or sayings of Jesus that created difficulty for the early church (e.g., Jesus' baptism by John the Baptist). Unfortunately, there are not many clear-cut cases of such embarrassment in the gospels, and our view of what would be an embarrassment might be significantly different than the early church's view (170).

The *criterion of discontinuity* (dissimilarity) focuses on words or deeds of Jesus that cannot be derived either from

Judaism at the time of Jesus or from the early church after him (e.g., Jesus' rejection of voluntary fasting for his disciples). But we do not have a full picture of first-century Judaism or Christianity, and this criterion creates a caricature of Jesus by divorcing Jesus from his Jewishness and from the church that followed him (171–74).

The *criterion of multiple attestation* focuses on sayings or deeds found in more than one independent source and/or form. The more witnesses and modes of witness, the more likely a word or deed comes from the historical Jesus (e.g., the message of the kingdom of God/heaven; 174).

The *criterion of coherence* is used after other criteria have generated enough historical material to indicate whether additional deeds or sayings echo items in the "established data base" (e.g., additional sayings about the kingdom of God; 176).

The *criterion of rejection and execution* recognizes that any account of Jesus' life and teachings must demonstrate why he was crucified by the Romans as "king of the Jews" (177).

Meier suggests that only a careful use of a number of criteria in tandem with each other, with allowance for mutual correction, can produce convincing results. Other secondary criteria, such as traces of Aramaic, Palestinian environment, and vividness of narrative, are much more problematic and should only be used to reinforce impressions gained from the five primary criteria (182–84).

Roots of the Person

During the latter part of the reign of Herod the Great, Jesus was born in Nazareth. His mother was Mary; his presumed father was Joseph (222). Jesus had at least four brothers—James, Joses, Jude, and Simon—and at least two sisters, and Meier notes that Jesus' relatives all bear names from patriarchs, the exodus from Egypt, or the entrance into the promised land. He postulates that Jesus' family thus could have shared in a reawakening of Jewish national and religious identity that looked forward to the redemption of Israel in its "full glory," an echo of which can be seen in Jesus naming twelve apostles as a possible symbol of national restoration (208).[5]

Meier sees Jesus as coming "out of a peasant background" but not being "an ordinary peasant" (278). Jesus ranked somewhere at the lower end of the "vague middle," not knowing the grinding destitution of the dispossessed farmer, the city beggar, the rural day laborer, or the rural slave (282): "Jesus grew up and conducted much of his ministry in an uncommonly peaceful oasis sheltered from the desert whirlwind that was most of Palestinian history" (351).

Conclusion

Meier's first volume is methodical, rigorous, and cogently argued. To most scholars, his conclusions are both unremarkable and traditional. The endnotes demonstrate that he has read widely, but unfortunately Meier limits his dialogue and cuts off investigations in some areas, such as any possible information gleaned from noncanonical sources or the extent of Hellenization evident in the gospels. Although Meier's fictional conclave consists of a Roman Catholic, Protestant, Jew, and agnostic, the language and content of this volume indicate that Meier is primarily in dialogue with Christian piety in general and Roman Catholic tradition in particular.

Meier's primarily text-based analysis (e.g., his use of Tacitus) leads him astray when he claims that Jesus worked in an "uncommonly peaceful oasis" in the lower end of the middle on the socioeconomic scale. This overly sanguine view needs to be corrected with the archaeological evidence of Antipas's commercialization and urbanization of Galilee, which caused significant strains on the vast majority of people in the surrounding countryside. The integration of anthropology and archaeology brings us closer to Jesus' historical situation: He most likely was more "marginalized" than "marginal."

Meier's use of the term *marginal Jew* itself is problematic. The term is intentionally vague, but it also domesticates Jesus and makes him "safe" for traditional Christianity. As Steven Cory notes, scholars often stress Jesus' Jewishness in ways in which they themselves, as Christians, are comfortable. In a similar way, they stress Jesus' "marginality" when it serves to support traditional Christianity.[6]

Volume II: *Mentor, Message, and Miracles*

To distill the insights of this 1,118-page volume into a few pages is not just daunting; it is impossible. This "long and dusty road" with a "prolonged, wearisome trek" through the miracle tradition (967), however, is worth the trip.

Meier divides the book into three parts: *Mentor* deals with John the Baptist; *Message* discusses Jesus' proclamation of the kingdom of God; *Miracles* investigates Jesus as wonder-worker. The three sections flow into each other, because key elements of Jesus' preaching and praxis are a continuation of and/or a response to John's preaching and praxis, and Jesus' miracles are one way in which he distinguished himself from John.

Meier presents John the Baptist as an ascetic Jewish prophet who proclaimed an imminent fiery judgment. Repentance and baptism were the only ways to avoid this judgment administered by a vaguely defined "stronger one" (27–40). Jesus' baptism by John implies that Jesus recognized him as a prophet and agreed with his imminent eschatology and message of repentance (109–10). Jesus probably became a member of John's inner circle, from which he perhaps gathered some of his own disciples (122, 129).

John remained Jesus' mentor, but Jesus publicly emerged in ways that differed from John. Jesus uttered fewer threats of doom and more good news of God's kingly rule, which was already powerfully at work in Jesus' healings and exorcisms, as well as his welcoming tax collectors and sinners into table fellowship

(132–33). In contrast to Crossan, however, Meier sees this as a shift of emphasis, not a rejection of John's message: Throughout his ministry, Jesus continued John's imminent eschatology, call to repentance, and baptism (154).

Meier unpacks crucial aspects of how John must have responded to Jesus' "more palpable and widespread success": John was facing death, Jesus was becoming successful, and God had not (yet) vindicated John's proclamation of imminent judgment. Meier notes John's poignant message to Jesus from prison: "Are you the one who is to come or are we to wait for another?" (Matt 11:3/Luke 7:19–20). Jesus responds by pointing to his activities that highlight his shift of focus: The healings and proclamation of good news to the poor are signs that a loving and merciful God was already acting to save Israel through the ministry of Jesus. Although Meier tries to soften Jesus' jarring response to John with words such as "discreet" and "delicate," he admits it is "shocking to see this implicit threat aimed at the Baptist": "And blessed is anyone who takes no offense at me" (Matt 11:6/Luke 7:23; 135–36). We never hear John's final response.

The Kingdom of God as Future

The kingdom of God was central to Jesus' preaching, and Meier examines five significant blocks of Jesus' sayings—from a variety of sources, major strands, and forms. These sayings demonstrate that Jesus proclaimed the definitive coming of God in the near future to establish God's rule (e.g., "your kingdom come" of the Lord's Prayer follows a trajectory launched by Ezekiel; 291). Yet unlike other eschatological prophets, Jesus did not set a timetable for the kingdom's appearance. Meier also makes a compelling argument that even if all of the future Son of man sayings were inauthentic, other passages amply demonstrate that Jesus expected an imminent end of the world.

The Kingdom of God as a Present Reality

In addition, Jesus' sayings indicate that in "some sense" the kingdom is already present in his words and deeds (350–51). This makes Jesus a more complicated and puzzling figure, because he proclaimed both a future and a present kingdom (e.g., Luke 17:21). The "star witness" for the present kingdom, Meier claims, is Luke 11:20: "If by the finger of God I cast out the demons, then the kingdom of God has come upon you" (399). Meier believes that this saying illustrates where Jesus was "unusual, if not unique," because he integrated the roles of exorcist, moral teacher, gatherer of disciples, and eschatological prophet all into one person (407). The "finger of God" is a bold affirmation that Jesus stands alongside Moses and Aaron as empowered by God to perform miracles that symbolized God's direct, concrete, and dramatic intervention (see Exod 8:12–15; 411).

How are these future and present aspects of the kingdom to be reconciled? Meier suggests that our modern, Western concern with logical consistency "might have been greeted with a curious smile by the Nazarene and his audience." On the other hand, Meier argues that the real answer to this "paradox" may be that the kingdom of God is a multifaceted reality: God's liberating power on behalf of Israel is already being experienced by those who encountered it in Jesus (452–53). In addition, Jesus' powerful preaching and teaching, especially the riddle-like parables, confronted his listeners with a kingdom of God that challenged their present ways of thinking and living. Through the parables, people experienced the kingdom as present in their everyday lives (1043).

Miracles

The miracles attributed to Jesus are essential to his portrait and, for the crowds that followed him, were the most striking element of his ministry (1044).[7] Jesus was the prophet who was accomplishing what John and the biblical prophets had foretold, and the kingdom of God was present, palpable, and effective in his miracles. Meier, though, considers the historian's task to be limited to whether "Jesus performed extraordinary deeds deemed by himself and others to be miracles" (630). In this light, Meier analyzes the miracle stories under four rubrics:

Exorcisms. The data for exorcisms are meager. Meier concludes, however, that such stories as the demon-possessed boy (Mark 9:14–29) and the reference to Mary Magdalene's exorcism (Luke 8:2) probably go back to historical events in Jesus' ministry. Other stories are likely later Christian creations, such as the Syrophoenician woman in Mark 7:24–30, a story created to exemplify the missionary theology of the early church (661). In my view, though, Meier is too hasty in reaching this latter conclusion. Jesus addresses "a sincere petitioner" with "harsh, insulting language" (660), but this harsh response most likely reflects an event in the ministry of Jesus, one which reflects the animosity that many Galileans felt toward Syrophoenicians.[8]

Healings. Almost every gospel source portrays Jesus as a healer. The healing of blind Bartimaeus (Mark 10:46–52), for example, was "reworked by Christian theology," but it is one of the strongest candidates for the report of a specific miracle going back to Jesus: A direct recipient of healing is named, tied to a specific place (outside Jericho) at a specific time of year (just before Passover), during a precise period in Jesus' ministry (his final trip to Jerusalem). It also includes two Aramaic phrases, as well as an "archaic conception" of Jesus as Son of David (690).

Raising the Dead. Meier, once again, limits himself to a narrow question: Do these stories "rest upon" actual events in Jesus' life, where he and other people *believed* that he had raised someone from the dead (775)? The raising of Jairus' daughter (Mark 5:21–43), Meier argues, is one such story. The story has a lengthy tradition history, an unusual mentioning of a petitioner's name and his status as a synagogue ruler, indications of a Semitic substratum (especially the Aramaic *talitha koum*), and the absence of any christological title (787). What happened exactly? Meier can only say that the story evidently goes "back to some action of the historical Jesus" (788).

The So-Called Nature Miracles. Meier denies that most of these stories have their basis in Jesus' ministry. The story of the temple tax question (Matt 17:24–27), for example, where Jesus instructs Peter to catch a fish and pay the tax with the coin in its mouth, was created in the context of the dispute about whether Jewish Christians should pay the temple tax (883). Likewise, the cursing of the fig tree (Mark 11:12–14, 20–21) is a Christian interpretation of the temple "cleansing." Neither story has a claim to go back to the public ministry of Jesus (884, 895).

Meier places all but one of the nature miracle stories into the "twilight zone of *non liquet*": They "appear to have been created by the early church to serve various theological purposes" (970). The only exception is the story of Jesus' feeding the multitude, which is most likely based on a symbolic meal that Jesus celebrated with a crowd by the Sea of Galilee, a meal that was "perhaps" interpreted as miraculous only later by the early church (968).

Conclusion: Miracles. Meier's analyses of the miracle traditions are *traditional* but not *conservative*. For example, he believes that virtually every element of the story about Jesus changing water into wine at Cana (John 2:1–11) is either a later creation or raises significant historical problems (e.g., the six massive stone jars at the house). Meier sifts carefully through the evidence and is not afraid to argue that not only were some of these materials shaped, but also some were created by the early church and/or the gospel authors. He does not stray far, however, from the academic mainstream, whether in his judgment of sources (e.g., Markan priority) or in the scholars with whom he interacts. Meier's works contain few if any idiosyncratic positions, and one wonders whether that illustrates his inability to envision other possibilities of text and context.

Second, Meier often chides some (primarily) American scholars for domesticating Jesus, for creating a Jesus palatable to university professors, for creating and "selling" a relevant historical Jesus for public consumption. Yet many scholars singled out by Meier—such as Marcus Borg—are just as willing as Meier to portray Jesus as performing healings. Domestication is a double-edged sword: Meier is understandably reluctant to conclude that these so-called nature miracles reflect historical events in Jesus' ministry. I do not contest his conclusions, but are those decisions influenced by the fact that, for him and most of his audience, nature miracles are among the most problematic traditions to accept as historical? Perhaps, in some ways, Meier also creates a more "palatable" Jesus for his modern audience, one that is influenced by Meier's own presuppositions.

Conclusion: Volume II

Meier concludes that Jesus' miracles supported, dramatized, and actuated his imminent eschatological message. The miracles also furnish an important clue concerning who people thought Jesus was and perhaps even to Jesus' own self-understanding. Regular miracle-working by an itinerant prophet active in northern Israel would conjure up thoughts of Elisha and Elijah. Jesus was "clothed in the aura of Elijah," the eschatological prophet "par excellence." Whatever his perceived relation to the Elijah of old, Jesus acted as the eschatological prophet who proclaimed the imminent coming of God's rule, and he made God's rule a present reality through his miracles. Jesus also taught ethical imperatives (e.g., love and forgiveness) and gave his followers concrete instructions on how to observe the law of Moses. It was this "convergence and configuration" of different traits in one person that gave Jesus his distinctiveness and made his roles "extremely dense and complicated" (1045–46).

Meier's lengthy volume sifts through a tremendous amount of data, but in some ways it is not as comprehensive as it appears. Meier's reconstruction of first-century Judaism, for example, seems too narrow, which regretfully leads him to accuse other scholars of creating a "non-Jewish" Jesus.

Meier's work has been well received in some quarters, but it has not (yet?) garnered the amount of attention that one would expect for a project of this size, scope, and depth. Partly this may be due to the "long and dusty road" down which only a few are willing to travel. Another reason may be that the book is *too* traditional, that the use of criteria, methodology, arguments, and dialogue partners represents more of an affinity with the New Quest rather than the current quest(s).[9]

As I read Meier's biting critiques of the Jesus Seminar and some of its members, I could not help but reflect on whether Meier's approach is all that different from theirs. Meier places emphasis on different sources, uses different variations of criteria for authenticity, and so forth, but the weighing and sifting of evidence is similar. He functions, however, as a committee of one, envisioning his work as that hypothetical unpapal conclave of four. Meier could gain much from the insights of others outside of his primary frame of reference, in a real dialogue with, for example, the social, cultural, and economic aspects of first-century Galilee that are essential to understanding Jesus and his contemporaries.

Volume III: *Companions and Competitors*

As a charismatic religious leader, Jesus' status and impact were determined by a web of social relationships with other individuals and groups in Palestine (2). In this volume, Meier focuses on those relationships.

Jesus in Relation to His Followers

Meier groups the followers of Jesus into three overlapping clusters: the outer circle of crowds, the middle circle of disciples whom Jesus called to follow him, and the inner circle of the Twelve, who were specifically chosen by Jesus to symbolize his (and their) mission to the twelve tribes of Israel (5).

Crowds. Jesus' preaching and teaching drew large crowds. This ability to attract crowds probably lasted throughout his entire ministry, although Jesus' complaints about "this generation" (e.g., Mark 8:12, 38) indicate that their enthusiasm did not always translate into deep, enduring commitment (29–30).

Disciples. From these ever-shifting crowds, Jesus probably drew some members into a more stable, smaller group, the "middle circle" of *disciples*—followers and pupils who would absorb his message and praxis. For these followers, Jesus seized the initiative—in the model of Elijah calling Elisha—by calling people to follow him (48, 50). They followed Jesus physically to experience and proclaim the kingdom of God; in doing so, they risked danger and hostility, even from their own families whom they left behind (69). Jesus' disciples had to be absolutely committed to him and his mission, and this group included devoted women followers who accompanied Jesus on his journeys around Galilee and to Jerusalem (76). Within this circle of disciples, Jesus taught special prayer forms, observances, and beliefs that marked them off as an identifiable group within first-century Judaism. Meier also surmises that a number of Jesus' supporters did not leave their homes and family. These supporters may have been healed or exorcised by Jesus, for example, and responded by offering food and lodging when he visited their villages (80–81).

The Twelve.[10] This inner circle became the "standing exemplar" of what it meant to be Jesus' disciple, and it served as a prophetic symbol of the regathering of the twelve tribes of Israel. Jesus, the eschatological prophet wearing the mantle of Elijah, addressed the people of Israel, and the Twelve's mission was one more prophetic step toward the reconstitution of eschatological Israel (248). Here Meier kicks against the goad of how to make Jesus relevant for modern Christians: Meier's reconstructed Jesus "was a failure." He addressed, challenged, and tried to regather the whole of Israel in the expectation of the imminent end. He was wrong, and he failed (289).

Jesus in Relation to Competing Jewish Groups

Meier examines other Jewish groups with which Jesus competed directly or indirectly (290):

Pharisees. The Pharisees enjoyed a reputation for their exact interpretation and practice of the law, and multiple attestation in the sources leads Meier to conclude that Jesus and the Pharisees probably debated such issues as Jesus' radical view on divorce. In his role as an eschatological prophet, it is also likely that Jesus offered some prophetic woes against Pharisees who rejected his message. Yet Jesus and the Pharisees shared many views, and the Pharisees had nothing to do with Jesus' death.

Sadducees. This group of elites consisted primarily of aristocratic priests who lived in Jerusalem. They relied on their wealth, their influence in many of the high priestly families and the running of the temple, and the support of the Romans to keep their hold upon power (637). Jesus' one interaction with Sadducees focused on the resurrection, which the Sadducees denied, and Jesus affirmed. The Sadducees, Meier claims, could not help but be "unnerved" by Jesus' claim to authority as the eschatological prophet with direct knowledge of God's will (639).

Essenes and other groups. The New Testament says nothing directly about Jesus' relation to or interaction with the Essenes and/or Qumran (489). Both Jesus and the Essenes, though, held eschatological hopes shaped by a tension between the "already" and the "not yet." They shared an ethical radicalism that flowed from their intense eschatological expectations, although Jesus' only true ascetic practice was his celibacy (634–35). Finally, Meier believes that very little can be said about Jesus' relation to other first-century groups, such as his interaction with or views about the Samaritans (549).

Conclusion

A full evaluation of Meier's contribution must await his fourth and final volume.[11] Certainly, Meier can be praised for attention to detail, and this contribution to the Anchor Bible Reference Library series will serve, no doubt, as a valuable reference book. His thorough analyses are reminiscent of the historical-critical works of such luminaries as Raymond Brown and Joseph Fitzmyer.

Unfortunately, over the course of these three volumes, Meier has become even more dismissive of some other historical Jesus scholars, especially those "lionized in recent years by the American media," who, in his opinion, do not truly acknowledge the Jewishness of Jesus. Meier also dismisses recent, more innovative approaches, sometimes with unneeded disdain. Even more problematic are the times Meier seems to challenge other scholars' academic integrity or honesty (e.g., III, 145). This negative and sometimes sarcastic tone diminishes Meier's credibility and highlights his subjectivity, no matter how even-handed his discussions might otherwise appear to be. The works of those scholars do have limitations, but so does his approach. For example, his overreliance on literary evidence—most of which was written by the elite in society—leads him to evaluate first-century Palestine "from above." Was Galilee "relatively tranquil" during the time of Jesus' ministry? Tacitus—an elite Roman author—tells us the entire empire was "basically quiet under Tiberius" (III, 622–23). Would a first-century Galilean Jew struggling to survive under Roman and Herodian oppression have the same opinion? Almost certainly not. Archaeological evidence, as well as the eruption of movements such as the ones of John the Baptist and Jesus, indicates that social and economic pressures were much higher than Meier admits.

Meier's detailed analyses give an illusory appearance of comprehensiveness. He conforms closely to the traditional canons of historical-critical approaches, but we must admit the inherent limitations of historical-critical criteria. Can multiple attestation, dissimilarity, and the other criteria give us an adequate reconstruction of Jesus? As Steve Bryan notes, many of Meier's historical judgments could "easily go the other way."[12]

In addition, Meier's traditional historical-critical insistence that to do comparative analysis there must be "exact" (or "real") parallels (159–60) is problematic. A lack of an "exact parallel" indicates that there may not be direct influence(s), but it should not discourage us from looking for broader socio-cultural patterns, conventions, and comparative texts.

Because Hellenistic culture influenced all Diaspora Judaism and Palestinian Judaism to a certain extent, the Jewishness of the synoptic Jesus does not preclude the existence of certain Hellenistic elements. A careful reading makes clear that the gospels merge biblical patterns with Hellenistic patterns and conventions. Meier, for example, compares Jesus' calling disciples to Elijah calling Elisha. What Meier overlooks, however, is that many of the teacher/disciple dynamics between Jesus and his disciples in the gospels stem from Hellenistic culture and are not found in the biblical tradition before the Hellenistic period.[13]

Finally, Meier's conclusion that Jesus was received and possibly presented himself as the Elijah who was expected to return to restore Israel is explicitly contradicted by passages in the gospels (e.g., Matt 11:14; 17:12; Mark 9:13; Luke 1:17). Meier has not adequately addressed this problem, but, then, another volume awaits us.

7
The Eschatological Prophet
of Social Change

> Jesus' freedom towards the Torah is based in wisdom and
> eschatology....His ethic, which intensifies and relaxes the
> Torah, is a programme aimed at the restoration of Israel; it
> seeks to preserve the identity of Israel in relation to the Gen-
> tile environment and inwardly to make possible the integra-
> tion of marginal groups. But this ethical programme has its
> *Sitz im Leben* in a group of itinerant charismatics around
> Jesus, who claimed to be renewing and representing Israel.[1]

Recent studies of the social and cultural contexts of the first-
century Mediterranean have made significant contributions to
New Testament scholarship.[2] Many social and cultural elements
found in ancient literature are not usually self-evident to modern
readers, so numerous aspects of the Jesus traditions are incompre-
hensible without an understanding of the social and cultural
processes that helped create and influence those traditions.

Gerd Theissen: Jesus the Apocalyptic Charismatic Miracle-worker

Over thirty years ago, Gerd Theissen helped pioneer the
social-historical approach to the study of Jesus and the transmission

of the Jesus tradition.[3] He argued that Jesus gave no fixed, written form to what he said, so the survival of oral tradition about him was dependent upon the interests, concerns, and some sort of sociological continuity between him and the people who transmitted his sayings (35).

This sayings tradition is characterized by an "ethical radicalism" based on the teachings of Jesus, a wandering charismatic who required a renunciation of home (Matt 8:20), family (Luke 14:26), and possessions (Mark 10:17–25). This uprooting of people from their homes illustrates a crisis within Jewish-Palestinian society.[4] After Jesus' death, his ethical radicalism continued in at least one group of early Christians, and these wandering charismatics' social situation is thus comparable to the social situation of the historical Jesus (45). They also preached a similar message—healings for the present and eschatological proclamation about the future—and were supported by various sympathizers in towns and villages. These sympathizers were most likely on the fringes of society, the poor and the hungry, people who would not be "upset" by the itinerants' preaching of the imminent end of the world (50–51). The synoptic tradition, in fact, is one of the few places in ancient literature where these oppressed poor have a voice; history is usually written by the "winners" and the elite in society (52).

Sociology of Early Palestinian Christianity[5]

Theissen's *Sociology of Early Palestinian Christianity* demonstrates how social analysis informs our understanding of early Christianity. Theissen attempts to describe typical social attitudes and behavior within the "Jesus movement"—the renewal movement within Judaism started by Jesus of Nazareth and existing in Syria and Palestine between 30 and 70 CE—and to analyze the Jesus movement's interaction within Jewish society in Palestine (1).

Theissen builds upon his earlier work by arguing that the internal structure of the Jesus movement was determined by the interaction of (a) the ethical radicalism of wandering charismatics who gave up home (Matt 8:20), family (Mark 10:29), possessions (Matt 10:10), and protection (Matt 5:39); (b) their sympathizers in the local communities who offered them material support; and (c) the Son of man, with whom the wandering charismatics identified. The wandering charismatics called by Jesus shaped the earliest traditions and provide much of the social background for the tradition of Jesus' words (10).

During this era, Palestine was in a constant state of crisis. Many people were "socially rootless" (e.g., resistance fighters, Essenes, and wandering charismatics), and "ordinary people" were threatened with debt and a decline of fortunes (45). Significant tensions existed between city and country, especially after the upsurge in the building of cities in the Hellenistic period (56–58). Significant frictions also existed between the various structures of government—the Jewish aristocracy, the Herodians, and the Romans. These political tensions created a breeding ground for radical theocratic movements that longed for the (imminent) kingdom of God (76). Theissen thus makes a significant contribution by situating the Jesus movement in its *context*— one of the differing responses to the crises in first-century Palestine. Thus other Jewish groups (e.g., Essenes, Pharisees) are seen in context as well, not just as *background* for the study of the Jesus movement.

Theissen argues that the Jesus movement articulated a vision of love and reconciliation to heal this deep-seated crisis in Palestinian-Jewish society (97–98). Jesus hoped to renew society from within, beginning with his small group of "outsiders" (110). As a renewal movement within Judaism, however, the Jesus movement failed, primarily because growing tensions in Palestinian Jewish society led to a return of traditional patterns of behavior and negative effects in Palestine due to Christianity's later success outside of Palestine (e.g., in which uncircumcised Gentiles were accepted into Christianity; 112–13). Although Jesus' vision of love and reconciliation was born in a society rent by crises, there was no chance of realizing that vision within that fractured society (118).[6]

Theissen's book was a bold, insightful approach to the study of the Jesus movement. Any pioneering work, however, has limitations. Freudian psychology, for example, rears its anachronistic head in various parts of the book: The wandering charismatics "worked off their aggression" (13) or the scapegoat assumed the "aggressiveness of the drives of the Id and that of the strictness of the super-ego" (109). Theissen also tends to assume that the wandering charismatics were only male disciples (e.g., 12, 15), an omission he corrects in later works.[7] The basic fact that Jesus and many of his first followers were itinerant charismatics, however, has survived the test of time.[8]

John H. Elliott observes that Theissen's trailblazing work demonstrates that the Jesus group is comprehensible only in terms of the entire social reality of which it was a part.[9] Theissen uncovered latent patterns of social structure, behavior, and areas of tension implicit in the sources, and he demonstrated how religious traditions help define social roles, values, and norms. The next essential step, Elliott argues, is an investigation of that reality through a systemic analysis of the entire social system and its "subsystems." The vast array of Theissen's data revealed tensions within society that would be more cogently explored with a sociological theory of conflict (as Theissen himself notes; 94), not Theissen's structural-functionalist sociological theory. The crisis was a product of political domination, economic exploitation, social destabilization by Rome, and by the diversified strategies of "domestic interest groups" (20–21). Elliott suggests that Jesus' approach did not function to restore "equilibrium" of the "system"; it spoke instead to the needs of the displaced, dispossessed, and marginalized people (22).

The Shadow of the Galilean[10]

Theissen's *The Shadow of the Galilean* integrates history and fiction in a poetic way that puts flesh on the bare bones of historical scholarship. This historical novel combines fictional characters (e.g., the main character Andreas) and fictional representations of historical personages (e.g., Pontius Pilate).

Andreas, a wealthy grain merchant from Sepphoris, is arrested by the Romans after an anti-Roman demonstration in Jerusalem. Although he is innocent of any wrongdoing, Andreas is blackmailed by Pilate into providing him with information about various groups within Palestine. One of his assignments is to investigate Jesus of Nazareth.

When Andreas takes his investigation to Nazareth, he discovers that Jesus is disrupting society (e.g., let the "dead bury the dead"), that Jesus' teachings reflect the contempt of the poor inhabitants of the land for the rich city-dwellers (75), and how traditions about Jesus were developed through oral tradition.

Andreas eventually concludes that Jesus was comparable to the Cynic itinerant philosophers who traveled around the country without a fixed abode, possessions, or profession. Even though loving God and one's fellow human beings, including one's enemies, were the two most important commandments (130), Andreas realizes that Jesus' proclamation of the kingdom of God was "revolt and rebellion" (131). Jesus also railed against oppression and exploitation, and he criticized the temple and its officials. This "peasant poet" enriched Jewish literature with marvelous parables, but he also was a unique prophet of an oppressed people (140) who preached an imminent judgment through a "mysterious man" (136).

The Shadow of the Galilean provides an excellent portrait of Jesus and his contemporaries by introducing the historical contexts and methodological issues involved in the study of the historical Jesus. Andreas also illustrates how scholars have to reconstruct the historical Jesus based on various sayings and traditions they "hear from others" (83). Since *Shadow* is a novel, other books are needed to fill in various historical gaps, but this book provides a good introduction to the historical Jesus.

The Gospels in Context[11]

During the 1980's, Theissen became more interested in archaeology and "cultural geography" and how those disciplines could be applied to the study of the historical Jesus and the history of the synoptic tradition (2). For example, he suggests that Jesus' comment about a "reed shaken by the wind" (Matt 11:7) is an implicit contrast between John the Baptist (who was not a "wavering reed") and Herod Antipas (who was). This wavering reed image for Antipas most likely stems from a coin he minted, which "very probably" has a reed image on it (29). Antipas also wavered like a reed between two capitals (Sepphoris and Tiberias) and two wives (Phasaelis and Herodias). The tradition in Matthew 11:7 thus most likely came from Jesus, who, like John, was an uncompromising prophet on a collision course with Antipas (41).

Theissen also persuasively argues that Jesus' insulting response to the Syrophoenician woman (the "dogs" of Mark 7:24–30) represents the bitterness that existed between Jews and Gentiles in the border regions between Tyre and Galilee (65).[12] The Syrophoenician woman is a relatively affluent hellenized Phoenician who comes to a Jewish prophet in the rural territory belonging to Tyre (70–71). Tyre was a rich island city that depended on food imports. This resulted in a struggle over food where the rural Jewish population in Galilee "usually got the short end of things" (75). Jesus' rude reply to the woman's request to heal her daughter (Mark 7:27) reflects the typical anger of Jewish peasants who suffered because they produced food for those rich city-dwellers while they themselves lived in want. Jesus believed that the poor Jewish people in Galilee should have enough food before providing food for the rich Gentiles in the cities (74–75, 79).[13]

The Historical Jesus: A Comprehensive Guide

In this book, Gerd Theissen and Annette Merz situate Jesus within the local, social, and political history of first-century

Judaism (ix). They believe, even with the problems inherent in our sources, that the form of Jesus' language can be known with a high degree of probability and "the totality of the form of Jesus' language shows his individuality clearly" (110). The portrait of Jesus in the gospels reflects elements of the post-Easter Jesus, but pre-Easter recollection of Jesus "stubbornly persists" as well (99–100). The "sociological continuity" between Jesus' lifestyle and the early Christian itinerant charismatics, for example, provides some continuity in Jesus' sayings (although they were reshaped; 106).

Theissen and Merz recognize that the synoptic traditions appear to be more reliable historically, but that extracanonical materials provide new insights into the processes by which traditions about Jesus were transmitted. These insights could also lead to a re-evaluation of synoptic traditions themselves (61). So Theissen and Merz strike a via media between scholars such as Sanders who utilize the synoptic traditions almost exclusively and scholars such as Crossan who place some extracanonical materials at an earlier and therefore privileged level.[14]

Theissen and Merz propose the *criterion of plausibility* to replace the criterion of dissimilarity: Traditions about Jesus that are plausible within Jesus' Jewish context and also provide a plausible explanation for later effects on Christian history "pass" the criterion of plausibility.[15] Whatever helps to explain the influence of Jesus and at the same time can have come into being only in a Jewish context is "historical" (116). The "plausibility" of a tradition is partly evaluated by multiple attestation in the sources as well as by the criterion of coherence (which is no longer dependent upon the methodologically suspect criterion of dissimilarity). Jesus can only have said and done things that a first-century Jewish charismatic could have said and done (118).

Although I disagree with aspects of their reconstruction of the historical Jesus, Theissen and Merz, in my view, still provide the best overall portrait to date. In brief, their "short life of Jesus" is as follows:

Jesus was born in Nazareth shortly before the end of Herod the Great's reign. He was the son of Joseph, an artisan in wood and stone, and his wife, Mary (153–55). He received an elementary Jewish education, was familiar with the great religious traditions, taught in synagogues, and was called "rabbi" during his public activity (354–56).

In his 20's Jesus joined the movement of John the Baptist, was baptized, and confessed his sins. Like John, Jesus expected the imminent judgment of God, but he saw that the imminent end preached by John was not yet materializing. After John was arrested, Jesus probably regarded the ongoing time as grace.[16] So Jesus struck out on his own with a related message, but one that put more emphasis on the grace of God that allows more time for repentance and gives everyone a chance.

Jesus traveled through Palestine as a homeless itinerant preacher with a focus on the small towns and villages northwest of the Sea of Galilee. He chose twelve disciples who represented the twelve tribes of Israel with whom he would "rule the Israel that soon would be restored" (217, 570). Jesus was unusual in that he also had women among his followers—a striking number of them, sometimes in unusual roles—including Mary Magdalene, who held a special position (219–25).

Jesus believed in the Jewish God who would soon bring deliverance to the poor, weak, and sick. He proclaimed the saving message of God's rule as both imminent and as already present (240). The announcement of salvation was at the center of his preaching; everyone had a chance to escape the coming judgment, including toll collectors and sinners (265).

The kingdom of God stood at the center of Jesus' preaching; healings and exorcisms formed the center of his activity. People flocked to this charismatic healer, and he saw these healings as signs that the kingdom of God was already beginning. From the early stages of his public activity, people attributed incredible things to him; his miracles both impressed and provoked his contemporaries (281). In contrast to other ancient miracle-workers, though, Jesus' healings and exorcisms are given an eschatological significance: "As an apocalyptic charismatic miracle-worker, Jesus is unique in human history" (309).

Jesus' ethical teaching intensified the universalist aspects of the Jewish Torah but dealt in a "liberal" way with ritual aspects that distinguished Jews from Gentiles. His vision of the future kingdom of God included Jews and Gentiles sharing a great meal, no longer divided by the commandments about food and purity. Jesus combined elements from both wisdom and eschatology in his ethics, but, as a good Jew, all his teachings remained grounded in the Torah—with the commandment to love God and neighbor at the center (348, 381). He radicalized this ethic, however, by demanding that love be shown to one's enemies, strangers, and outcasts. In addition, he called for a radical ethic of freedom from family, possessions, home, and security (353–54). A distinctive feature of the Jesus tradition is that the powerless, persecuted, and humiliated are to show an "aristocratic ethic of responsibility": the generosity and renunciation of power that God demands from the powerful. This behavior is not a passive surrender to evil, but an active, nonviolent resistance of the powerless with the aim of revealing injustice and overcoming it (343, 393).

Jesus' public activity included several "symbolic actions": choosing and sending out the Twelve, eating with toll collectors and sinners, the entry into Jerusalem, and the public action in the temple (431). Eating with toll collectors and sinners led to disputes with Pharisees, but that did not result in any deadly hostility. Instead, it was Jesus' criticism of the temple, his prophecy that God would replace the old temple with a new one, and his actions against it in Jerusalem that provoked the aristocracy and led to his death (433). The night he was arrested, Jesus ate a simple farewell meal with his disciples in which he instituted a new rite in celebration of a "new covenant" with God and in expectation of the imminent confrontation with the authorities (436). He probably hovered between expecting death and the hope that God would intervene before his death to usher in God's kingly rule. The aristocracy arrested him because of his temple action but accused him before Pilate of being a royal pretender (467). Many people, including some of his followers, expected Jesus to become the royal Messiah who would lead Israel to glory. Before Pilate, Jesus himself did not deny that expectation, because he was convinced that God would bring about the great turning point of history. Jesus was thus condemned and crucified with two bandits. His male disciples fled, but some women disciples witnessed the crucifixion from afar (571–72).

After his death, Jesus first appeared either to Mary Magdalene (which is more probable) or Peter, and then to several disciples together (497–99). They became convinced that he was alive. Their expectation that God would intervene had been fulfilled differently than they had expected, so they had to reinterpret Jesus' mission: He was the *suffering* Messiah and the future "man" from Daniel 7, to whom God would give all power. Jesus thus took a place alongside God, and this messianic Judaism only gradually separated from its mother religion later in the first century (572).

A critical aspect of Theissen and Merz's reconstruction is that Jesus combined two elements that seem to stand in "insuperable tension": wisdom and eschatology (373). They correctly argue that these two currents of tradition are already united within Judaism: God becomes accessible through Wisdom as well as "extra-normal visions" independent of temple and Torah. So both traditions are available for Jesus to interpret and transcend the Torah (374). The ethical preaching of Jesus thus corresponded precisely to three sources of Jewish ethics: the Torah at the center (read in the prophetic spirit), with Wisdom and eschatology alongside it (381).

Theissen's Quest Continues

Theissen's *A Theory of Primitive Christianity* attempts to describe "primitive Christian religion."[17] He argues that a "theology" of early Christianity is not enough; since the "dynamic of primitive Christian faith is rooted in the dynamic of life," we must investigate the semiotic, social, psychological, and historical contexts in which early Christians lived (1).

Theissen envisions "religion" as a cultural sign language with a semiotic, systemic, and cultural character that promises a gain in life by corresponding to an ultimate reality. First-century Judaism, for example, was governed by the basic axioms of exclusive monotheism and covenantal nomism (13).[18] Christianity kept the first axiom of Judaism but replaced covenantal nomism with faith in a redeemer.[19] The religious sign system thus is restructured in light of the figure of a single redeemer who stands alongside God (13).

Jesus began this process by "revitalizing" the Jewish sign language. Jesus lived, thought, and worked as a Jew, and he combined the idea of the kingly rule of God (a political metaphor) with the image of God as father (a family metaphor). Both images come from Judaism, but Jesus "demilitarized" the myth by speaking about the reign of God but never of God as "king." It is God as father and God's kingdom, as the Lord's Prayer demonstrates: "Our father, your kingdom come" (23–24).

Jesus "historized" this myth by combining it with his own history—the kingdom was present in his words and actions (24). It led him to give poetic expression in his parables to a new perception of God. Through his "demilitarizing" of this kingdom, he detached it from the hope for victory over the Gentiles, but he did not "depoliticize" the kingdom. His calling of the Twelve, his entry into Jerusalem, and his actions in the temple, for example, are all inherently political acts: The turning point in history toward the kingdom of God was imminent, and, in fact, already beginning (37).

Theissen thus concludes that Jesus was a Jew who stood at the center of Judaism and began a renewal movement within it. His itinerant lifestyle and ethical radicalism made him a "marginal Jew" only from the perspective of other Jewish groups. Even his words and actions against the temple focused on reforming the temple by replacing it with a new, eschatological temple (33).

The rest of this "tour de force"[20] focuses on the development of early Christianity, but Theissen's discussion of Jesus' eschatology leads him to discuss briefly what he had concluded in his earlier article, "Jesus—Prophet einer millenaristischen Bewegung?"[21] ("Jesus, a Prophet of a Millenarian Movement?"). Theissen argues that such millenarian movements usually develop when there is a conflict of two cultures. One culture is politically superior, and people in the "inferior" culture hope for a fundamental change in their situation (197–98). Theissen compares and contrasts the Jesus movement with three other millenarian movements (e.g. the *Kimbanguismus* in Central Africa; 207) and concludes that the Jesus movement overcame frontiers that other millenarian movements usually do not surmount. Christianity arose during a period of a clash between two highly differentiated "equal" cultures (Roman and Jewish). The Jesus movement is also distinct because it was successful in overcoming the imperialistic alien culture (when the Roman emperor Constantine converted to Christianity), it was open to other cultures rather than antagonistic to them, and the message of Jesus was not syncretistic—it was rooted within Judaism (227–28).

William R. Herzog II: *Jesus, Justice, and the Reign of God*

William Herzog's social-scientific approach to the historical Jesus is influenced by his participation in the Context Group—a group of scholars dedicated to utilizing the social sciences to help interpret the New Testament's texts and contexts. Herzog's *Parables as Subversive Speech,* for example, provides a detailed analysis of the social setting of Jesus' parables, and it utilizes Paolo Freire's "pedagogy of the oppressed" as an interpretive lens through which to view them. Jesus' parables focused, Herzog argues, not primarily on the vision of the glory of the reign (kingdom) of God, but on the gory details of how oppression serves the interests of a ruling class. Parables explore how human beings could respond to break the spiral of violence and the cycle of poverty created by such exploitation (3).[22]

Jesus, Justice, and the Reign of God[23]

Herzog's "historical Jesus" is the Jesus whose public work can be reconstructed through historical analysis and with historical imagination.[24] *Jesus, Justice, and the Reign of God* places Jesus in the context of an aristocratic Roman Empire and a peasant society within an advanced agrarian society. Herzog proposes social-scientific models for understanding systemic relations in agrarian societies, such as the relationship between city and countryside. Since our information from the first century is limited, these models allow us to "screen old information through new lenses" (31–32). Herzog also argues that we must examine our preexisting "gestalt" of the historical Jesus before proceeding to utilize any "criteria for authenticity," because that preexisting image of Jesus will have an unacknowledged influence on how we apply those criteria. Due to the fragmentary nature of the materials in the synoptic tradition,[25] all interpreters need to propose a holistic image (paradigm) that captures their hypothesis about the historical Jesus. Once we posit that hypothesis, we can then test it by analyzing the Jesus tradition in light of the first-century Palestinian context (41–43).

Herzog's hypothetical paradigm is that Jesus was a prophet of the justice of the reign of God. As a peasant prophet, Jesus interpreted the Torah through the "little tradition" found in the countryside of Galilee, not the "great tradition" that emanated from the Jerusalem elite. He spoke to those Galileans who, like him, were increasingly separated from their land and tradition by Roman domination, Herodian exploitation, and the elite's control of the temple. Jesus was a prophet who continued the paradigmatic work of Moses and the other great prophets in Israel's past by interpreting the social, economic, and political situation in light of the covenant promises of Yahweh. To this tradition, Jesus added his distinctive voice and functioned also as a teacher and healer (70).

Herzog believes that Jesus' temple action was an enacted parable that symbolized the temple's impending destruction but not its restoration. Jesus did not envision a new temple, because it was an "oppressive institution" that represented the policies of the ruling class. The temple tax contributed to the economic oppression of Galilean peasants, and the entire system of the temple's economic exploitation concentrated even more wealth in the hands of a wealthy few. In its role as a bank, Herzog posits, some of the vast temple funds were used by the temple's wealthy elite to make loans to rural peasants. In practice, these loans functioned in a predatory way; they garnered money from exorbitant interest rates, or they served as a means of obtaining a peasant's land through foreclosure. Either way, the peasants suffered, and the wealthy elite prospered (137).

The elite who ran the temple claimed to be the sole brokers of Yahweh's patronage, but Jesus explicitly challenged their role. He declared that God chose him as "Son of man" to broker God's blessings and offer forgiveness and healing: God rejected the temple priesthood and opened an alternative way to God through Jesus (131).

Jesus' action in the temple makes this more explicit. In light of the temple's economic oppression, Jesus declares, "You have made the temple a cave of social bandits" (139). By attacking the moneychangers and sellers of doves, Jesus attacked essential operations in the collection of the temple tax and integral parts of the temple sacrificial system. Since Jesus saw himself as the broker of God's forgiveness, he believed that the temple was no longer necessary.

For Herzog, Jesus' inclusive table fellowship also rejected the priestly model for purity and acted out a different vision for Israel. Instead of interpreting the Torah through the lens of the "purity code," the priestly way of structuring society, Jesus interpreted the Torah via the "debt code," the protections that God's law extends to prevent the ruling class from exploiting the poor (156–57). Jesus' command to the rich man in Mark 10:17–22, for example, demonstrates that Jesus read the Torah as a demand for the justice of the reign of God. The Torah is about the distributive justice of God, a God who gave the land as a gift to be shared equitably (166–67).

Jesus' view of the temple and the ruling elite was dangerous, especially if he had a large following. Jesus was not a lone voice crying in the wilderness of Herodian oppression; he was a prophet of God speaking with authority, gathering disciples, challenging the evils of the reign of the Romans, Herodians, and priestly aristocracy, and announcing the coming justice of the reign of God (203–5).

Herzog argues that Jesus, though, went further than claiming the role of a prophet. Jesus' healings and exorcisms mediated God's power (209), and he acted as the broker of God's justice, covenant favor, and forgiving love. As the agent of God who reconstituted the people of God, he embraced people on the margins and brought them home. This community of God was based on "generalized reciprocity," an open sharing based on generosity and need. In this way, the Galilean villages could become more aligned with the values and practices of the reign of God (213–16).

Jesus' potential threat to the political/religious authorities led to his arrest, "show trial," and predetermined death. The Roman ruling elite and the small group of Jewish aristocrats in Jerusalem held a firm grip on power, and Jesus' death demonstrated what horrors awaited anyone who challenged their authority. A small group of women, though, remained "looking from afar" as Jesus died on the cross. Herzog, *pace* Crossan's hypothesis that Jesus' body probably was devoured by scavengers, argues that the women were there precisely to protect the body: "It was their final act of piety" (246). Herzog also believes that Jesus' resurrection defines the relationship between the historical Jesus and the risen Christ: The resurrection is God's way of saying, "My kid got it right. Go thou and do likewise" (250).

Prophet and Teacher

In *Prophet and Teacher,* Herzog summarizes his hypothesis about Jesus' public identity (12):

Jesus was a prophet in the tradition of Israel's prophetic figures. Jesus, like his prophetic predecessor Moses, interpreted the Torah and mediated between Yahweh and the people. In Jewish tradition, prophets spoke on behalf of those who had been silenced, marginalized, and oppressed by the ruling elite. Jesus was also in the prophetic tradition of Elijah and Elisha, who were known for their mighty acts as well as their words. So Jesus' words and mighty deeds, although distinctive, "revived the prophetic voice" and "renewed the prophetic act" (12–14).

Jesus was a teacher and rabbi, a subversive pedagogue of the oppressed. Like Paolo Freire, Jesus functioned as a pedagogue of the oppressed: He advocated for the peasants of Galilee, and his teaching attempted to alter the balance of power. The apocalyptic imagery of Jesus, for example, envisioned a transformed world, and his pedagogy encouraged peasants to break their "culture of silence" and to reimagine their world (15–19).

Jesus was a traditional healer and exorcist, a shamanistic figure. Jesus' healings and exorcisms reveal that he was concerned about healing both disease (the physical problem) and illness (the social consequences of disease). Jesus' actions thus led to the restoration of those healed with their family and community (e.g., the healed Gerasene demoniac is told to "go home to your friends"; Mark 5:19).

Jesus was a reputational leader who brokered the justice of Yahweh's covenant and coming reign. These mighty works confirmed Jesus' role as a reliable broker of God's power and blessings: It was by the "finger of God" that he cast out demons and brokered the reign of God (Luke 11:20). In the context of Roman rule, Herodian domination, and the exclusive claims of the priests in the temple to be the brokers of God, Jesus' claim was subversive and threatening, because he challenged both the view of the

Torah held by the leaders in Jerusalem and also the temple system itself, which was beholden to the Romans (22–24).

How does this view of Jesus impact Herzog's interpretation of the gospels? His ingenious reading of the parable of the Laborers in the Vineyard (Matt 20:1–16) is a good example. Unlike the interpreters who argue that the owner of the vineyard symbolizes God's gracious, generous goodness, Herzog believes that Jesus' parable sets up a direct confrontation between two extremes of agrarian society: an exploitative landowner and poor desperate peasants fighting a losing battle for survival. Such wealthy landowners were the very ones who, through usurious loans and the resulting foreclosures, deprived poor peasants of their family's small parcels of land and forced them into a lethal, landless form of poverty.

Jesus' parable exposes this exploitation for what it actually is: an abrogation of God's law, misuse of God's land, and victimization of the poor. It also illustrates the incongruity between the coming reign of God and the earthly systems of oppression that pretend to be legitimate guardians of the values of God's law. For Herzog, Jesus exposed the contradictions between the injustice under which Jesus' fellow peasants lived and the justice demanded by the Torah of God.

Herzog's work is a refreshing social-scientific approach that sheds much light on the first-century contexts in which Jesus lived and worked. It also convincingly demonstrates how religious, economic, and political concerns were interconnected. How often would it occur to modern readers in the United States, for example, that Jesus' admonitions about adultery and divorce (Matt 5:27–32)—areas of disruption in village life—are less about sexual ethics and more a critique of property rights?[26]

Herzog's "paradigm" has much to commend it. On the other hand, a paradigm should be a general framework, not a procrustean bed into which every saying or action of Jesus should be forced. Herzog's overall view is often compelling, but sometimes the data appear to be massaged to fit into a rigid "pedagogy of the oppressed" model. That does not take away from Herzog's insights, but it does cause some questioning of his exegesis of certain passages (e.g., does he underestimate Mark's contribution to the Sabbath controversy in Mark 1:21–28?). Overall, however, Herzog's work is a powerful reminder of the oppression that first-century Galilean peasants faced in their daily lives.

To Be Continued

Due to the vast amount of historical Jesus research, this volume, even more than other *WATSA?* volumes, has focused on a limited number of voices that have dominated discussions. To my chagrin, many voices thus, by necessity, have been excluded. I mention some here briefly, in the hope that future dialogues will be more inclusive and then future reviews of scholarship can include them as well.

Elisabeth Schüssler Fiorenza recently noted that "no book-length feminist study on the Historical-Jesus has been published."[27] Yet much has been written about the role of women within the early Jesus movement. Schüssler Fiorenza, for example, argues that Jesus' first followers were "*Jewish wo/men...* [who] followed a vision of liberation for every wo/man in Israel."[28] This "emancipatory movement," as a discipleship of equals, most likely understood itself as a "prophetic movement of Sophia-Wisdom" (89–90). What Schüssler Fiorenza correctly realizes, but does not completely avoid herself, is that the popular portrait of the "Jesus the Feminist" egalitarian who stands against "Jewish" patriarchal systems is inherently anti-Jewish and misguided.[29] More recent studies suggest that there were "moderate liberative tendencies" at work in the first century, but that they did not originate with Jesus. Greater social freedom for women appears already to be happening in the greater Roman Empire.[30] Kathleen Corley thus argues that the "limited participation" of women among Jesus' disciples or table companions does not necessarily differentiate Jesus from a Greco-Roman or Palestinian environment, and it most likely does not reflect "an egalitarian aspect of his teaching."[31] That debate about the Jesus movement will continue, hopefully in a wider context.

Other voices that deserve to be included in future dialogues are studies of Jesus from a non-Western perspective. Africa, for example, contributes a historical Jesus that is "unabashedly confessional," a Jesus "who will help the church in Africa."[32] Engagement with African scholars and contexts provides important new areas of dialogue, including the image of Jesus as life-giver and healer, the one who fulfills the aspirations for life in Africa and who restores life wherever it has been diminished.[33] Jesus is also envisioned as the divine conqueror, one who is victorious over the spiritual realm, evil forces, and thus becomes the protector, liberator, and leader.[34] A particularly important contribution is the image of Jesus as a "loved one," a member of a family and community who "actually shared in the life of the people."[35] This perspective is a much-needed corrective for Western scholars who still overlook the family/group-oriented nature of Jesus' first-century historical context.

Engagement with these and forthcoming studies will allow us to reconstruct a historical Jesus in better and more meaningful ways, especially in light of the similarities between biblical cultural contexts and African contexts. I look forward to those dialogues.

Conclusion

Much has been gained through social and cultural studies of the historical Jesus, and much remains to be done. Yet these studies also accentuate a paradox: Jesus becomes more understandable, but, for some, he also becomes more alien and distant. We receive partial glimpses, however, important glimpses that sometimes include the "voices of the silenced," but even these glimpses demonstrate the cultural divides between then and now.

Yet, as Carolyn Osiek observed, for non-Western persons, the cultural contexts may now be more familiar, once the Western, post-Enlightenment framework inherent in much New Testament study is illuminated and (partly) dismantled.[36] For those who are interested, the challenge remains: How to modernize Jesus authentically without anachronizing or domesticating him? Pieces of the puzzle will still be missing; different people and different eras may place the pieces of the puzzle in different places; the historical Jesus will remain delightfully and frustratingly enigmatic. But these social and cultural analyses provide additional pieces of the historical Jesus puzzle that allow us to see the first-century world and Jesus a bit more clearly.

Conclusion

When Jesus turned and saw them following, he said to them, "What are you looking for?" They said to him, "Rabbi... where are you staying?" He said to them, "Come and see" (John 1:38–39a).

Historical Jesus scholarship remains a creative, dynamic, and exciting area of research, with longstanding debates being approached in new ways. These debates include what sources should be used to reconstruct the life and teaching of Jesus and how they should be used. Should we focus on the synoptics, the connections between Q and Thomas, or include other non-canonical sources? How historically reliable are those sources? Should the burden of proof be on authenticity, inauthenticity, or on whoever is making the argument? What criteria or methodology should we use, and which criteria, if any, should have priority? How can we integrate various disciplines in our methodologies, and which disciplines are appropriate and most useful?

Although Jesus was a Jewish first-century teacher and wonder-worker, our sources about him are written in Greek. What type of Jew was Jesus? The Jesus portrayed in the gospels speaks and acts in roles that combine Jewish and Hellenistic modes of speech and action.[1] How can we best integrate Jesus' words and deeds to reconstruct a more complete portrait? Where do we start in our evaluation? With words, deeds, and/or a hypothetical "gestalt" of Jesus?

A major debate also still rages over how much of a role, if any, did apocalyptic/eschatological elements play in the teaching of Jesus. I suggest that any portrait of the historical Jesus must come to terms with Jesus as both an apocalyptic prophet and a prophet of social and economic justice for an oppressed people. Any portrait that does not integrate both these aspects generates a caricature of Jesus of Nazareth.

What relevance does this Jesus, this foreign, enigmatic figure have for us today? Too often, he is domesticated, and, as Albert Schweitzer noted, the "great imperious sayings" lie "in the corner like explosive shells from which the charges have been removed."[2] This first-century Jewish eschatological prophet of social change is foreign to us in many, many ways. Yet, through the centuries, central elements of his voice still ring clear. The kingdom of God proclaimed by Jesus, for example, mirrors in many ways the hierarchal and patriarchal systems of his day, but it also provides a devastating critique of those systems: Jesus demands higher standards in the present in light of the imminent eruption of the kingdom of God, higher standards by which all social systems can be evaluated.[3]

These higher standards include vertical generalized reciprocity, the redistribution from the advantaged to the disadvantaged that expects nothing in return (e.g., Luke 14:1–24). They include giving to everyone who begs from you and being merciful as God is merciful (Luke 6:29–30, 36). They include not only calling Jesus "Lord, Lord," but also doing what he taught (Luke 6:46). These higher standards also include reaching out to people across boundaries of class, ethnicity, gender, culture, or any other barriers that human beings erect between themselves. And, finally, they include working in love for justice and peace, reaching out to people who are victims not only of disease, hunger, and poverty, but who also are victims of oppressive systems.[4] Jesus, we must never forget, was a prophet of an oppressed people, who lived his life as a poor peasant artisan suffering under Roman and Herodian oppression in first-century Galilee. Jesus' life and ministry were focused on proclaiming and inaugurating the kingdom of God among and for the poor, demonstrating God's mercy, love, and compassion. Jesus also proclaimed and demonstrated that the powerless should not passively surrender to evil, but resist it actively and nonviolently, revealing injustice and overcoming it.[5] As Jon Sobrino notes, this Jesus is liberation and good news for the poor and for all those who seek to be human in this world; it is in that interaction that we encounter the "real" Jesus.[6]

No matter the historicity of the event itself, the Lukan Jesus dialogically echoes the authentic voice of the historical Jesus (and the prophet Isaiah) when he proclaims release to the captives, good news for the poor, and announces that the oppressed should go free (Luke 4:16–21). An essential element of hearing Jesus' voice is rediscovering that peasant-artisan prophet of an oppressed people who proclaimed a message of hope for the poor as well as a message of judgment upon the wealthy who exploit (or ignore) them. Jesus truly did comfort the afflicted and afflict the comfortable.

Why should we take the effort to search for Jesus and to reconstruct his message? This effort is fascinating on a purely historical level, but Charles Hedrick suggests another very important reason for Christians to ponder:

> The savior worshiped in song and prayer seems so easy to understand…[but] studying Jesus, rather than simply affirming creedal statements learned in childhood, can bring new insights, a broader understanding, and a deeper appreciation for the complementary relationship between faith and history.[7]

Many Christians, at first, discover that academic reconstructions of the historical Jesus can be disconcerting if not troublesome for their faith. In the long run, however, such efforts most often lead to a more authentic, robust, and mature faith. The historical Jesus still challenges our hearts, minds, and imaginations, and, as we search for "where he is staying," he is there before us, dialogically inviting us to "Come and see...."

Notes

Preface

1. Gerd Theissen, *The Shadow of the Galilean: The Quest of the Historical Jesus in Narrative Form* (trans. John Bowden; Philadelphia: Fortress, 1987), 95.

2. A point made by Robert J. Miller, *The Jesus Seminar and Its Critics* (Santa Rosa, CA: Polebridge, 1999), 74–76; and William Arnal, *The Symbolic Jesus* (Oakville, CT: Equinox, 2005).

3. Albert Schweitzer, *The Quest of the Historical Jesus* (trans. Dennis Nineham; Minneapolis: Fortress, 2001), xiii.

4. This quote from the journalist Finley Peter Dunne (1867–1936), originally about the role of newspapers, is often echoed by my colleague, Hoyt Oliver, to describe his role as a professor of religion.

5. See Thomas Merton, "Blessed Are the Meek: The Roots of Christian Nonviolence," *Fellowship* 33 (1967): 18–22.

Chapter One: The Modern Quest for the Historical Jesus

1. Gerd Theissen, *The Shadow of the Galilean: The Quest of the Historical Jesus in Narrative Form* (trans. John Bowden; Philadelphia: Fortress, 1987), 98–99.

2. The German comes from the title of his book, *Der sogenannte historische Jesus und der geschichtliche biblische Christus,* which was first published in 1892. The quote comes from the English translation, *The So-Called Historical Jesus and the Historic Biblical Christ* (trans.

145

C. E. Braaten; Philadelphia: Fortress, 1964). Kähler begins his essay by saying, "I regard the entire Life-of-Jesus movement as a blind alley," and continues by stating, "The historical Jesus of modern authors conceals from us the living Christ." The crux of Kähler's argument is that "The real Christ, that is, the Christ who has exercised an influence in history, with whom millions have communed in childlike faith, and with whom the great witnesses of faith have been in communion...this Christ is the Christ who is preached....The person of our living Savior." The above quotes come from the reproduction of Kähler's initial 1892 essay found in Gregory W. Dawes, *The Historical Jesus Quest* (Louisville: Westminster/John Knox, 1999), 216, 234.

3. See C. J. den Heyer, *Jesus Matters: 150 Years of Research* (Valley Forge: Trinity Press International, 1997), 52.

4. Marcus Borg, *Jesus in Contemporary Scholarship* (Harrisburg, PA: Trinity Press International, 1994), 195. As Borg also notes, these two conceptions live in a both/and dialogical relationship instead of existing in an either/or binary choice between opposites. Borg goes on to argue that these terms lessen the dichotomy between the two conceptions, do not privilege the "Christ of faith," and suggest that the "Christ of faith" is not immune from developments in historical scholarship.

5. John Dominic Crossan, *The Birth of Christianity* (San Francisco: HarperSanFrancisco, 1998), 39. Crossan was responding to the critique of the Jesus Seminar in general and his work in particular made by Luke Timothy Johnson, *The Real Jesus* (San Francisco: HarperSanFrancisco, 1998).

6. James D. G. Dunn, *The Theology of Paul the Apostle* (Grand Rapids: Eerdmans, 1998), 183, 188.

7. Likewise, the Nicene Creed skips from the virgin birth to Jesus' death and resurrection: "...For us and our salvation he came down from heaven, was incarnate of the Holy Spirit and the Virgin Mary and became truly human. For our sake he was crucified under Pontius Pilate; he suffered death and was buried. On the third day he rose again in accordance with the Scriptures; he ascended into heaven and is seated at the right hand of the Father. He will come again in glory to judge the living and the dead, and his kingdom will have no end...." I am using the versions of the Apostles' Creed and Nicene Creed that are found in the *Book of Common Worship* (Louisville: Westminster/John Knox, 1993), 64–65.

8. For a summary of this "traditional" view, see Clinton Bennett, *In Search of Jesus* (London: Continuum, 2001), 70–90. The *Diatessaron* of Tatian, a harmony of the four gospels, perhaps is the best symbol of this early view of the synchronicity of the pre-Easter and post-Easter Jesus. The focus on Jesus' birth, death, and resurrection continued through the Reformation. As N. T. Wright notes in his discussion of the sixteenth-century Reformers: "For many conservative theologians, it would have been sufficient if Jesus had been born of a virgin (at any time in human history, and perhaps from any race), lived a sinless life, died a sacrificial death, and risen again three days later." See N. T. Wright, *Jesus and the Victory of God* (Minneapolis: Fortress, 1996), 14.

9. For a brief but excellent introduction to these issues, see Gerald R. Cragg, *The Church & the Age of Reason, 1648–1789* (New York: Penguin Books, 1970).

10. Noted by Bennett, *In Search of Jesus,* 90–91. As Dawes points out, however, the pioneering work of Benedict Spinoza first outlined the program for a historical study of the Bible, and he argued for its importance in his *Tractatus Theologico-Politicus* (Chapter 7: "Of the Interpretation of Scripture"). See Dawes, *The Historical Jesus Quest,* 2–3. Dawes also provides an excerpt from the *Tractatus Theologico-Politicus* (5–26).

11. In addition to the primary texts, I am also utilizing in this chapter the summaries of the quests found in W. Barnes Tatum, *In Quest of Jesus* (revised and enlarged edition; Nashville: Abingdon, 1999); James D. G. Dunn, *Jesus Remembered* (Grand Rapids: Eerdmans, 2003); Borg, *Jesus in Contemporary Scholarship;* Wright, *Jesus and the Victory of God;* Mark Allan Powell, *Jesus as a Figure in History* (Louisville: Westminster/ John Knox, 1998); den Heyer, *Jesus Matters;* and others. It is surprising how many current commentators still depend on and basically follow the outline of the Quest found in Albert Schweitzer, *The Quest of the Historical Jesus* (New York: Macmillan, 1968; originally published as *Von Reimarus zu Wrede,* 1906). Scholars tend to ignore, however, the significant additions made to the work in the second edition published in 1913: *Geschichte der Leben-Jesu-Forschung* (Tübingen: Mohr Siebeck, 1913). In his introduction to the 1968 translation of the first edition, James Robinson argues that the later additions were "laborious," "outdated," and in contrast to the first edition not "permanently relevant" (Schweitzer, *Quest* [1968], xxvii). On

the other hand, Dennis Nineham's introduction to the 1913 edition—
which was not translated into English until 2001—declares that "[t]he
changes added very considerably to the value of the work, and as long
ago as 1931 Schweitzer himself expressed his regret that the later English editions continued to be based on the original German one." See
Albert Schweitzer, *The Quest of the Historical Jesus* (trans. Dennis
Nineham; Minneapolis: Fortress, 2001), xiii. Unless noted specifically
as [1968], I am using the 2001 translation of Schweitzer's revised work.

12. Schweitzer, *Quest,* 24.

13. Woolston argued that the disciples of Jesus stole his body
from the tomb and lied about his resurrection. They later, however, came
to believe in the resurrection. See Colin Brown, *Jesus in European
Protestant Thought, 1778–1860* (Durham, NC: Labyrinth, 1985),
36–55. Reimarus picks up the theme of the disciples' theft of Jesus'
body and subsequent deception.

14. In 1627, Woolston, a professor at Cambridge, was sentenced
to a year in prison for denying the historicity of Jesus' miracles. He died
in confinement. See Brown, *Jesus in European Protestant Thought,* 42.
Thomas Aikenhead was hanged in Edinburgh in 1697 for claiming that
Ezra (and not Moses) authored the Torah. See Marcus J. Borg, *Jesus in
Contemporary Scholarship,* 185.

15. See *Reimarus: Fragments* (ed. Charles H. Talbert; Philadelphia: Fortress, 1970). Note also the differing evaluations of the importance of Reimarus by Schweitzer, *Quest,* who labeled the seventh
fragment as "one of the greatest events in the history of criticism" and "a
masterpiece of world literature" (15–16); and Dunn, *Jesus Remembered,*
who calls Schweitzer's view of the fragment "overblown" (29).

16. Tatum, *In Quest of Jesus,* 94.

17. Stephen Neill and Tom Wright, *The Interpretation of the New
Testament, 1861–1986* (2nd ed.; Oxford: Oxford University Press,
1988), 13.

18. David Friedrich Strauss, *The Life of Jesus Critically Examined*
(ed. Peter C. Hodgson; Ramsey, NJ: Sigler, 1994), xvi–xxiv. Norman
Perrin quite aptly called Strauss a "stormy petrel," or someone who
brings discord. See Norman Perrin, *Rediscovering the Teaching of Jesus*
(New York: Harper & Row, 1976), 211.

19. Dunn, *Jesus Remembered,* 33–34.

20. Ibid., 34.

21. The idea that one could even write a *biography*—in the modern sense of the word—of Jesus would soon be disputed. In that light, it is fascinating to compare Renan's work with the biography of Jesus (published in 2000) by Bruce Chilton—which includes insights of modern scholarship from archaeology, social customs, religious beliefs and practices, political forces, and other elements of the first-century Mediterranean world. See Bruce Chilton, *Rabbi Jesus: An Intimate Biography* (New York: Doubleday, 2000).

22. Renan's *Vie de Jésus* was originally published in 1863. I am using *The Life of Jesus* (New York: Random House, 1927). Renan, a Roman Catholic, rejected (traditional) Christian faith but was still fascinated by the historical Jesus. See Sean Freyne, *Jesus, A Jewish Galilean* (New York: T & T Clark, 2004), 8–9.

23. See John Haynes Holmes's introduction in Renan's *Life*, 18–19.

24. His fate was thus similar to Strauss's, and, as Schweitzer noted (*Quest*, 166–67), Strauss hailed Renan as a "kindred spirit and ally" and metaphorically "shook hands with him across the Rhine."

25. Schweitzer's description of Renan's work is almost as colorful: "He offered his readers a Jesus who was alive, whom he, with his artistic imagination, had met under the blue heaven of Galilee.... People's attention was arrested, and they thought they could see Jesus, because Renan had the skill to make them see blue skies, seas of waving corn, distant mountains, gleaming lilies, in a landscape with Lake Gennesaret for its centre, and to hear with him in the whispering of the reeds the eternal melody of the Sermon on the Mount" (Schweitzer, *Quest*, 159). Dunn calls Renan's work "luscious fruit" (*Jesus Remembered*, 37), whereas N. T. Wright considers it "charming but cloying": N. T. Wright, "Quest for the Historical Jesus," in *Anchor Dictionary of the Bible*, III:797.

26. Wright, "Quest," 797.

27. For example, Renan incorrectly claimed: "With its solemn doctors, its insipid canonists, its hypocritical and atrabilious devotees, Jerusalem has not conquered humanity....The North [Galilee] alone has made Christianity; Jerusalem, on the contrary, is the true home of that obstinate Judaism which, founded by the Pharisees, and fixed by the Talmud, has traversed the Middle Ages, and come down to us" (113). Cf. Freyne, *Jesus*, 9.

28. As Schweitzer noted about the work of Christian Hermann Weisse; Schweitzer, *Quest,* 111. N. T. Wright, however, believes that the idea that source criticism—as well as the later form and redaction criticisms—is part of the quest for the historical Jesus is one of the six "commonly held but erroneous views." See Wright, "Quest," 796.

29. Ernest Renan, in contrast, often preferred the Gospel of John to the synoptics in evaluating historicity.

30. Karl Lachmann, "De ordine narrationum in evangeliis synopticis," *Theologischel Studien und Kritiken* 8 (1835): 570–90. Shortly thereafter but independent of Lachmann, both Christian Gottlob Wilke and Christian Hermann Weisse voiced similar opinions.

31. H. J. Holtzmann, *Die Synoptischen Evangelien* (Leipzig: Englemann, 1863). The most influential argument in English for the priority of Mark came much later from B. H. Streeter, *The Four Gospels* (London: Macmillan, 1924).

32. As Norman Perrin noted, "Liberal scholarship, therefore, accepted the full burden of historical critical scholarship without hesitation and without reserve, believing that the historical core of the gospel narratives, when reached, would reveal Jesus as he actually was, and that he then would be revealed as worthy of all honour, respect and imitation, revealed as the founder of a faith which consisted in following him and his teaching closely and purposefully." Perrin, *Rediscovering,* 214.

33. Dunn, *Jesus Remembered,* 35. The essential goodness of human beings was supplemented by the belief—due to the influence of Charles Darwin's theory of evolution—that moral evolution is a natural continuation of the biological process to "higher forms of life" (36).

34. Albrecht Ritschl, *The Christian Doctrine of Justification and Reconciliation* (Edinburgh: T & T Clark, 1900).

35. Adolf von Harnack, *What Is Christianity?* (trans. Thomas Saunders; Gloucester, MA: Peter Smith, 1978).

36. "The Gospel, as Jesus proclaimed it, has to do with the Father only and not with the Son" (144).

37. See W. R. Matthews's introduction in *What Is Christianity?,* x.

38. Dunn, *Jesus Remembered,* 39.

39. Schweitzer, *Quest,* 6.

40. William Wrede, *The Messianic Secret* (Cambridge: James Clarke, 1971). The quote comes from the excerpt of *The Messianic Secret* that is found in Dawes, *The Historical Jesus Quest,* 114.

41. See John K. Riches, *A Century of New Testament Study* (Valley Forge: Trinity Press, 1993), 22–23.

42. Ibid., 23.

43. As Perrin notes, the collapse of the Liberal Quest for Jesus occurred in Germany, but it took another fifty years for this collapse to occur—and not totally—in Britain and the United States: Perrin, *Rediscovering,* 214–15. And, as a number of scholars make clear—Dunn, for example, calls it the *coup de grace* (*Jesus Remembered,* 51)—the most devastating blow to the optimism of Liberalism and thus to the Liberal Quest for Jesus was the bloody debacle of World War I.

44. Both Reimarus and Strauss had argued that Jesus proclaimed the imminent end of the world in which God would bring about dramatic change, but they believed that this eschatological message was primarily political. See, for example, Reimarus, *Fragments,* 217–18; Strauss, *Life of Jesus,* 294. As Reimarus declares: "It was then clearly not the intention or the object of Jesus to suffer and die, but to build up a worldly kingdom, and to deliver the Israelites from bondage [political oppression]" (150). Strauss also emphasizes the fact that this view of Jesus was consistent with Jewish expectations of the Messiah: "Now the fact is, that the prevalent conception of the messianic reign had a strong political bias; hence, when Jesus spoke of the Messiah's kingdom without a definition, the Jews could only think of an earthly dominion, and as Jesus could not have presupposed any other interpretation of his words, he must have wished to be so understood" (293). After further arguments to this effect, Strauss declares, "Hence it appears a fair inference, that Jesus himself shared the Jewish expectations which he here sanctions" (294).

Liberalism did not share these assumptions. Ritschl, for example, argued that the kingdom of God preached by Jesus was ethical in scope. The kingdom of God is "the highest good only in the sense" that it creates an ethical ideal. See Albrecht Ritschl, *Three Essays* (Philadelphia: Fortress, 1972), 222. This view is intimately connected to Immanuel Kant's categorical imperative and ideal commonwealth. See Benedict T. Viviano, *The Kingdom of God in History* (Wilmington, DE: Michael Glazier, 1988), 114.

45. Johannes Weiss, *Jesus' Proclamation of the Kingdom of God* (Philadelphia: Fortress, 1971). Weiss delayed publishing his analysis until 1892, three years after the death of Ritschl—Weiss's teacher and father-in-law!—but when published it produced a tempest. By 1927,

however, the idea that the kingdom of God was an apocalyptic concept in Jesus' message was widely accepted. See Norman Perrin, *Jesus and the Language of the Kingdom* (Philadelphia: Fortress, 1976), 35.

46. Albert Schweitzer, *The Mystery of the Kingdom of God* (trans. Walter Lowrie; New York: Macmillan, 1914; rpt. 1950), ix, 108–9.

47. Schweitzer's higher view of the accuracy of the traditions about Jesus, for example, even extended to the Sermon on the Mount: It was not a "composite speech" but "for the most part delivered as [it has] been handed down to us": Albert Schweitzer, *The Kingdom of God and Primitive Christianity* (New York: Seabury, 1968), 108–9.

48. Ibid., 103, 111.

49. Or as Schweitzer writes in *Kingdom:* "The death of Jesus thus brings about the coming of the Kingdom of God" (123).

50. As Schweitzer later notes (*Kingdom,* 128), he changed his view about the importance of Isaiah 53 from *Quest* (387–89).

51. And, in a passage changed in the 1913 edition: "But the truth is, it is not Jesus as historically known, but Jesus as spiritually arisen within men, who is significant for our time and can help it. Not the historical Jesus, but the spirit which goes forth from Him and in the spirits of men strives for new influence and rule, is that which overcomes the world" (1968: 401). Compare the revised text: "Our relationship to Jesus is ultimately of a mystical kind. No personality of the past can be transported alive into the present by means of historical observation or by discursive thought about his authoritative significance. We can achieve a relation only when we become united with him in the knowledge of a shared aspiration…and when we rediscover ourselves through him" (486).

A more famous example is Schweitzer's (unchanged) final "He comes to us as One unknown" paragraph in *Quest,* which also evokes elements of mysticism: "He comes to us as one unknown, without a name, as of old, by the lakeside, he came to those men who did not know who he was. He says the same words 'Follow me!' and sets us to those tasks which he must fulfill in our time. He commands. And to those who hearken to him, whether wise or unwise, he will reveal himself in the peace, the labours, the conflicts and the sufferings that they may experience in his fellowship, and as an ineffable mystery that they may experience in his fellowship, and as an ineffable mystery they will learn who he is…" (487).

52. See Robert J. Miller, ed., *The Apocalyptic Jesus: A Debate* (Santa Rosa, CA: Polebridge, 2001), 1.

53. This title, which I amended slightly, stems from the Haverford Library Lectures given by Henry J. Cadbury in April 1963, later published as *The Eclipse of the Historical Jesus* (Pendle Hill Pamphlet 133; Lebanon, PA: Sowers Printing, 1964).

54. Noted by Tatum, *Quest,* 98–99. As Bultmann wrote, "Jesus Christ confronts men nowhere other than in the *kerygma,* as he had so confronted Paul and brought him to decision. The *kerygma* does not mediate historical knowledge (of Jesus)…and one may not reconstruct the historical Jesus.…That would be the Christ according to the flesh of the past. Not the historical Jesus, but Jesus Christ, the preached Christ, is the Lord." Rudolf Bultmann, *Glauben und Verstehen* (vol. I; Tübingen: Mohr, 1933), 208. Quoted by Cadbury, *Eclipse,* 28.

55. Rudolf Bultmann, *Jesus and the Word* (New York: Charles Scribner's Sons, 1934; German edition, 1926), 8. See also Perrin, *Rediscovering,* 219–23.

56. Rudolf Bultmann, *History of the Synoptic Tradition* (New York: Harper & Row, 1963). This book was originally published in 1921.

57. The problems with this criterion are obvious—not least of all that the teachings of Jesus originate from within Judaism, and early Christianity is based to a large extent on his teaching.

But the criterion of dissimilarity has diminished in importance. See, for example, the evaluation by Gerd Theissen and Dagmar Winter, *The Quest for the Plausible Jesus: The Question of Criteria* (Louisville: Westminster/John Knox, 2002), which includes an appendix (261–315) with quotes from various scholars "on the general theme of the criterion" that begin with Martin Luther (1521) and end with Jürgen Becker (1996).

58. Dunn, *Jesus Remembered,* 76.

59. Noted by Tatum, *In Quest of Jesus,* 100.

60. See Dale C. Allison, Jr., "The Secularizing of the Historical Jesus," *Perspectives in Religious Studies* 27 (2002): 136. He is quoting E. F. Scott, "Recent Lives of Jesus," *Harvard Theological Review* 27 (1934): 1.

61. Allison, "The Secularizing of the Historical Jesus," 138.

Chapter Two: The Continuing Quest for the Historical Jesus

1. Günther Bornkamm, *Jesus of Nazareth* (New York: Harper & Row, 1960), 22.

2. W. Barnes Tatum, *In Quest of Jesus* (revised and enlarged edition; Nashville: Abingdon, 1999), 101. Four years later, Käsemann still argued that it was only through the proclamation of Jesus that we could encounter the historical Jesus. See Ernst Käsemann, "New Testament Questions of Today," in *New Testament Questions of Today* (trans. W. J. Montague; London: SCM, 1969), 12.

3. What Käsemann called "our only real and original documentation of him" (23). He, like many other scholars, ignored noncanonical sources.

4. Käsemann believed that the Gospel of John's "symbolism" did not put it in the same category as the synoptics, as far as the connection to "historical reality."

5. Ernst Käsemann, "Blind Alleys in the 'Jesus of History' Controversy," in *New Testament Questions of Today,* 35.

6. See Rudolf Bultmann, "The Primitive Christian Kerygma and the Historical Jesus," in *The Historical Jesus and the Kerygmatic Christ* (ed. C. E. Braaten and R. A. Harrisville; Nashville: Abingdon, 1964), 18.

7. Käsemann, "Blind Alleys." Käsemann reacts with less-than-judicious language by accusing Bultmann of "logical inconsistency" (42), "logical contradiction" (51), an "odd mixture of concessions and restrictions" combined with "an unremitting offensive" (52), more than one *"volte-face"* (54), an extraordinarily aggressive "counter-offensive" (55), and an "absolutely unacceptable" theological position (58).

8. James M. Robinson also notes "Bultmann's shift in position" in Robinson's *A New Quest of the Historical Jesus* (London: SCM, 1959), 19–22. In that section, Robinson argues that Bultmann had conceded that the message of the historical Jesus in some respects was already *kerygma* (20–21).

9. Published in Ernst Fuchs, *Studies of the Historical Jesus* (trans. A. Scobie; London: SCM, 1964), 11–31.

10. William R. Herzog II, *Jesus, Justice, and the Reign of God: A Ministry of Liberation* (Louisville: Westminster/John Knox Press, 2000), 15.

11. The essay was originally published as "Jesus Christus" in the third edition of the German Protestant encyclopedia, *Die Religion in Geschichte und Gegenwart* in 1959. It was revised, expanded, and translated into English as Hans Conzelmann, *Jesus* (trans. J. Raymond Lord; Philadelphia: Fortress, 1973).

12. As noted by Robinson, *New Quest*, 18. Perrin relates that Conzelmann's foray into the verbal jousting between Bultmann and his former students ended abruptly in 1959. During his inaugural lecture at Göttingen in 1959, Conzelmann announced that he found himself in complete agreement with Bultmann's response to his students in "The Primitive Christian Kerygma and the Historical Jesus," and that he would no longer participate in the discussions: Norman Perrin, *Rediscovering the Teaching of Jesus* (New York: Harper & Row, 1976), 265.

13. Robinson, *New Quest*.

14. James M. Robinson, "The Recent Debate on the Quest," *Journal of Bible and Religion* 10 (1962): 207.

15. Tatum, *Quest,* 102. Obviously, the use of existentialism to "bridge the divide" between the historical Jesus and the Christ of faith was less convincing to those scholars who did not accept existentialist presuppositions.

16. Käsemann, for example, spent several pages vigorously rebutting Jeremias's approach in Käsemann's famous "Blind Alleys" essay (24–35). Käsemann situated Jeremias's work firmly in the "Old Quest" category (24), accused Jeremias of using "over-simplified, ambiguous, and careless" reasoning (30), and declared that Jeremias's "dogmatic theology" discredited "the New Testament enterprise" (31).

17. Joachim Jeremias, *The Parables of Jesus* (rev. 2nd ed.; New York: Charles Scribner's Sons, 1972), 22.

18. His insights are also, not surprisingly, partly a reflection of his own rather conservative Lutheran piety. See David B. Gowler, *What Are They Saying About the Parables?* (Mahwah, NJ: Paulist, 2000), 8–10, 106–7; and Norman Perrin, *Jesus and the Language of the Kingdom* (Philadelphia: Fortress, 1976), 106.

19. Joachim Jeremias, *New Testament Theology: The Proclamation of Jesus* (New York: Charles Scribner's Sons, 1971), 2–3.

20. T. W. Manson, *The Teaching of Jesus* (Cambridge: Cambridge University Press, 1967).

21. Jeremias also agreed with Manson's thesis that Jesus envisioned the Son of man as a "corporate entity" (274; see Manson, *Teaching*, 211–34).

22. For Jeremias, Jesus' use of "Son of man" reflects its use in Jewish apocalyptic literature and in Daniel 7:13, where the Son of man will appear in divine glory, surrounded by hosts of angels, will sit at the right hand of God, and will judge all peoples (272). Jeremias believed that Jesus used it to refer to himself only in his future eschatological role. In the gospels, Jesus calls himself the *Son of man* sixty-five times, and the term is used in three different ways: (1) as a circumlocution for "human being" in which Jesus refers to himself in his ministry (e.g., Luke 7:34; 9:58; 19:10); (2) as a term that is used in predictions about his suffering and death (e.g., Mark 8:31; 9:12; 9:31; 10:33); and (3) in connection with a (his?) future apocalyptic role (e.g., Mark 8:38; 13:26; 14:62).

23. For a trenchant critique, see Gerd Theissen and Dagmar Winter, *The Quest for the Plausible Jesus: The Question of Criteria* (Louisville: Westminster/John Knox, 2002), as well as Leander Keck, *A Future for the Historical Jesus* (Nashville: Abingdon, 1971), who argued that we should search for the "characteristic Jesus" instead of the "distinctive Jesus" (33).

24. E. P. Sanders, *Jesus and Judaism* (Philadelphia: Fortress, 1985). Sanders was primarily interested in Jesus as a historical figure, as the title of his 1993 book indicates: E. P. Sanders, *The Historical Figure of Jesus* (London: Penguin, 1993).

25. The Jesus Seminar quickly became controversial—including its practice of voting on authenticity with colored beads, its conclusion that only about 20 percent of Jesus' reported words and deeds were historically probable, and its arguments for a nonapocalyptic Jesus. See Tatum, *Quest*, 103–4.

26. James H. Charlesworth and Walter P. Weaver, *Images of Jesus Today* (Valley Forge: Trinity Press International, 1994), xiii–xiv.

27. Tatum, *Quest*, 104, 109.

28. John Dominic Crossan, *The Historical Jesus: The Life of a Mediterranean Jewish Peasant* (San Francisco: HarperSanFrancisco, 1991), xxviii.

29. First suggested in Stephen Neill and N. T. Wright, *The Interpretation of the New Testament*, 1861–1986 (2nd ed.; Oxford: Oxford University Press, 1988), 379–403, and further delineated in Wright's *Jesus and the Victory of God* (Minneapolis: Fortress, 1996).

30. Wright, *Jesus,* 83–85.

31. Robert W. Funk, *Honest to Jesus* (New York: HarperCollins, 1996), 65.

32. Gerd Theissen and Annette Merz, *The Historical Jesus: A Comprehensive Guide* (trans. John Bowden; Minneapolis: Fortress, 1996), 10–11.

33. Adapted from William R. Telford, "Major Trends and Interpretive Issues in the Study of Jesus," in *Studying the Historical Jesus* (ed. Bruce Chilton and C. A. Evans; Leiden: Brill, 1994), 57–58.

34. Edgar McKnight, *Jesus Christ in History and Scripture* (Macon, GA: Mercer University Press, 1999), 223.

35. Sentiments similarly expressed by scholars such as Vernon K. Robbins, "Picking Up the Fragments: From Crossan's Analysis to Rhetorical Analysis," *Foundation and Facets Forum* 1:2 (1985): 31–64; and Paula Fredriksen, "What You See Is What You Get: Context and Content in Current Research on the Historical Jesus," *Theology Today* 52 (1995): 75–98.

36. John Dominic Crossan, *The Birth of Christianity* (New York: HarperCollins, 1998), 20.

37. Gowler, *Parables,* 38–39, 100–101.

Chapter Three: The Jesus Seminar and Its Critics

1. Robert W. Funk, *Honest to Jesus* (New York: HarperCollins, 1996), 11.

2. I have some albeit limited knowledge of the workings of the group. Two of my former professors were founding members ("Charter Fellows") of the Jesus Seminar. I myself joined briefly as a student member in 1987, to help me keep abreast of trends in historical Jesus research, but I never attended a meeting. My participation was limited to receiving via mail the seminar papers that were presented at the meetings, as well as copies of the Westar Institute's journal, *Foundations & Facets Forum.* I vaguely recall being given the opportunity once to "vote" by mail—no beads were involved!—concerning the authenticity of some sayings of Jesus, but I did not respond.

From 1990 to 1992, I also participated in a Westar Institute research team, an interdisciplinary group working on a new commentary series. Robert Funk came to our group's initial meeting at Emory University to describe the research project. I did not particularly share his entrepreneurial spirit, but the research group was a wonderful, collegial team, and the project seemed a worthy one. In 1992, during the SBL November meeting in San Francisco, all of us, however, withdrew from the project, and my (very limited) connection to the Westar Institute came to an end.

3. Robert W. Funk, Bernard Brandon Scott, and James R. Butts, *The Parables of Jesus: Red Letter Edition* (Sonoma, CA: 1988), 21.

4. Robert W. Funk, Roy W. Hoover, and the Jesus Seminar, *The Five Gospels: The Search for the Authentic Words of Jesus* (New York: Macmillan, 1993), 36.

5. Robert W. Funk and the Jesus Seminar, *The Acts of Jesus: The Search for the Authentic Deeds of Jesus* (New York: HarperCollins, 1998), 36.

6. Robert J. Miller, *The Jesus Seminar and Its Critics* (Santa Rosa, CA: Polebridge, 1999), 47–60.

A more colloquial form was published in *The Fourth R* 2:6 (1989): 1: Red: That's him; Pink: Sure sounds like him; Gray: Well, maybe; Black: There's been some mistake! No way!

For the "acts of Jesus," the categories were
- Red: The report is historically reliable
- Pink: The report is probably reliable
- Gray: The report is possible but unreliable; it lacks supporting evidence
- Black: The report is improbable; it is not congruent with verifiable evidence

The "consensus" of the Seminar was calculated with the voting results of the color-coded system: Each vote had a numerical equivalent (red = 3; pink = 2; gray = 1; black = 0). The Seminar counted the number of votes, and the number of votes in each color was multiplied by the corresponding value (e.g., the red votes were multiplied by three), and the sum was divided by the total number of votes (i.e., if thirty Fellows voted, the totals were each divided by thirty). The Seminar then decided the range of values that would signify their "consensus": red (2.251–3.0), pink (1.501–2.25), gray (0.751–1.5), or black (0.0000–0.75).

7. Against critics who complained that good scholarship is not decided by voting, Robert Miller argued that this idea stemmed from the

practice of biblical translation committees and from the United Bible Society committees that vote on critical editions of the Greek text of the New Testament (*The Jesus Seminar,* 66). The real objection seems to be the publicity generated by the Seminar and its method of voting; Luke Timothy Johnson, for example, notes that translation committees vote privately. See Luke Timothy Johnson, *The Real Jesus: The Misguided Quest for the Historical Jesus and the Truth of the Traditional Gospels* (New York: HarperCollins, 1996), 4. Miller suggests instead that part of the problem is that until now, biblical scholars have been able to keep "their secrets to themselves" (66). Miller has a point, although the hyperbole of a small number of the members of the Seminar made them an easier target.

8. Most of the Seminar's critics object to the Gospel of Thomas's inclusion as one of the "five gospels." Robert Miller responds that the Seminar recognized that Thomas reworked "a lot" of the material according to its theological tendencies, but that similar "reworking" was done in every gospel. The gnostic interpretations of the material, Miller argues, are "usually utterly obvious, almost hamfisted, and are easily detachable from earlier material" (*The Jesus Seminar,* 70). The major difference in believing that Thomas is an independent voice is that it then provides multiple (independent) attestation for sayings in the gospels that might otherwise be only singly attested.

9. "The Emerging Jesus," *The Fourth R* 2:6 (1989): 1, 11–15.

10. Two other papers on the "Kingdom of God" presented at that meeting were also important in this regard: Leif Vaage's "The Kingdom of God in Q," and Karen King's "Kingdom in the Gospel of Thomas." Since I am using original drafts of papers presented to the Seminar, not published versions, I will not quote from them directly.

Leif Vaage's paper argues that the kingdom of God in the formative stages of Q is an ethical expression that epitomizes and rationalizes the way of life of the people Q represents (the "poor"). Parallels to this usage are found not in apocalyptic literature but in the wisdom literature of the Hellenistic-Roman world, such as the Wisdom of Solomon and Philo, especially that of the Cynics, such as Dio Chrysostom. Vaage concludes that in Q Jesus is comparable to other teachers of wisdom and popular philosophers in the Hellenistic-Roman world, specifically the Cynics.

Karen King's paper similarly argues that Jesus' sayings about the kingdom were understood and transmitted by the community in a nonapocalyptic sense. The term *kingdom of God* is used as a means of self-definition and social formation to delineate boundaries — who is "inside" and who is "outside" — and to establish an ascetic community ethic. To accomplish this task, Thomas utilizes the language and mythology found in wisdom literature. King observed, however, that both the tendency to envision Jesus as a teacher of wisdom and the view of Jesus as the bearer of an apocalyptic, eschatological message were found in early Christian traditions.

11. As noted in *The Acts of Jesus,* 104–5.

12. For example, Jesus says, "Okay — you're clean!" in Mark 1:41, and in Matthew 23:13, he exclaims, "You scholars and Pharisees, you imposters! Damn you!"

13. Funk was even obliged to pen "Tongues of the Wise," a column of advice for how to respond to critics of *The Five Gospels.* Robert W. Funk, "Tongues of the Wise," *The Fourth R* 6:6 (1993): 2, 15. Funk argues that the Seminar's only goal was to discover and report the truth, and therefore they need not be apologetic, defensive, or rude in their responses to critics. Funk goes on to say that their "hostile" and "ideological" critics often include personal attacks and peripheral issues. Funk's advice is to put those critics on the defensive by asking pointed questions, such as whether the Jesus of history is to be distinguished from the Christ of faith/the creeds (2). Another key question to be asked was "Do you think Jesus believed that the world was about to end in his day? If you do, was Jesus mistaken on that point? On what other points was he mistaken?" This question strikes at a key problem for some of those who believe in an eschatological Jesus: Since the Jesus of the synoptics predicted the imminent end of the world, Jesus and/or the people writing those gospels was/were wrong.

See also Funk's assessment of the Seminar's conclusions in the same issue, "The Gospel of Jesus and the Jesus of the Gospels," 3–10.

Robert Miller denies that the Seminar ever claimed that their views reflected "a consensus among New Testament scholars" (*The Jesus Seminar,* 66). Miller, however, seems to downplay the sometimes flamboyant statements of some members of the Seminar.

14. Funk and the Jesus Seminar, *The Acts of Jesus,* 1.

15. Funk's introduction to the book offered five conditions that might have prompted early Christians to "employ their imaginations" to invent stories about Jesus: (1) to fulfill a prophecy or to match scriptural

language (e.g., John 19:32–37); (2) to "market" the Messiah to the larger world; (3) to express their own convictions about who Jesus was; (4) to justify practices adopted (later) by early Christians; (5) to buttress claims of authority about themselves or their leaders (6–8).

16. Funk lists the following "profile of the historical figure of Jesus" (based on their previous work on the sayings of Jesus) that the Seminar used to help evaluate reports of Jesus' behavior: Jesus (a) was itinerant; (b) rejected societal norms about "family ties"; (c) was accused of being demon-possessed; (d) performed exorcisms; (e) was perceived as a social deviant; (f) had an "entourage of undesirables"; (g) embraced the unclean; (h) took liberties with Sabbath observance; and (i) attracted crowds but had his critics (32–33). Jesus' sayings gave little support to his activities as a charismatic healer and no support to the idea that he could perform miracles in the natural world (33–34).

The Seminar also refined its voting system: Each vote still had a numerical equivalent (red = 3; pink = 2; gray = 1; black = 0), but now the Seminar decided that its "consensus" judgments would be reported as voting percentages: the range of values for red (above 75%), pink (50.01 to 75%), gray (25.01 to 50%), or black (25% and below). The advantage of this system, Funk argued, is that all votes count. One of the disadvantages is that black votes disproportionally pull down the average, but Funk averred that this feature was consonant with the "methodological skepticism" that was a working principle of the Seminar: "When in doubt, leave it out" (37).

17. Since the Seminar's "earlier strata" of the New Testament contain no appearance stories, it concluded that it did not seem necessary for Christians to believe the literal veracity of any of the later (resurrection) narratives (462; this statement seems to belie any claim to theological neutrality in their work; it also incorrectly excludes Paul from the earlier strata).

18. John Kloppenborg cautioned that the "layers" in Q should not be used "to imply anything about the ultimate tradition-historical provenance of any of the sayings." That is, some of the sayings in the secondary layer may be "older" than some of the sayings in the "earliest layer." See John Kloppenborg, *The Formation of Q* (Philadelphia: Fortress, 1987), 244–45. Likewise, Helmut Koester warns that "It is questionable…whether this early stage of Q can really be defined as noneschatological, even more doubtful whether one can draw from such

observations the conclusion that the preaching of the historical Jesus had no relation to eschatology": Helmut Koester, "Jesus the Victim," *Journal of Biblical Literature* 111 (1992): 7.

19. Funk argues that the image of Jesus as God's son developed in stages from Jesus being elevated to God's son at his resurrection (stage one; Rom 1:3–4), his baptism (stage two; Mark 1:10–11), his birth (stage three; the infancy narratives), and, finally, as the "pre-existent," divine *logos* (stage four; Phil 2:5–10; John 1:1–5, 14). Funk does not address the fact that this "fourth stage" is found in the earliest text he cites (Phil 2:5–10).

20. Funk's Jesus also tends to reflect values that can be easily applauded in today's society, such as Jesus being inclusive (199) and trampling "indifferently on the social dividers that enforced segregation" (202). Funk's portrayal of Jesus as a "provocative Galilean sage" is dependent in part on first-century Galilee being, in his words, "semi-pagan" (33) and "hellenized" (70), including the "presence of Hellenistic philosophers and teachers in Galilee during Jesus' life" (70). We are left once again with the question of exactly what does it mean to be a Galilean Jew in the first-century CE, with more specific questions about differences between inhabitants of Sepphoris, Tiberias, the small villages in Lower Galilee, or Caesarea to the south.

Although Funk's Jesus appears attractive, I must admit that my privileged position within a major university in the wealthiest industrialized nation in the world means that I would likely be a target of the "real" Jesus.

21. Marcus J. Borg, *Jesus: A New Vision* (San Francisco: Harper & Row, 1987).

22. Marcus J. Borg, *Conflict, Holiness, & Politics in the Teachings of Jesus* (Lewiston, NY: Edwin Mellen, 1984). See also Borg's "A Temperate Case for a Non-Eschatological Jesus," in *Jesus in Contemporary Scholarship* (Harrisburg, PA: Trinity Press, 1994), 47–68; originally published in *Foundations & Facets Forum* 2:3 (1986): 81–102.

23. Borg, "A Temperate Case," 54.

24. Marcus J. Borg, "Jesus and Eschatology: Current Reflections," in *Jesus in Contemporary Scholarship,* 88.

25. See Geza Vermes, *Jesus the Jew* (New York: Macmillan, 1973), 65–78, 206–13.

26. Elsewhere Borg labels Jesus as an "ecstatic" or "Jewish mystic." See, for example, Marcus J. Borg, "Jesus: A Sketch," in *Profiles of Jesus* (ed. Roy W. Hoover; Santa Rosa, CA: Polebridge, 2002), 130–33.

27. Marcus J. Borg, "Portraits of Jesus in Contemporary North American Scholarship," in *Jesus in Contemporary Scholarship,* 26.

28. Borg later revised this language to call Jesus a "movement catalyzer." See Borg, "Jesus: A Sketch," 135.

29. Borg is even more intentional about merging his roles as a "secular Jesus scholar" at a public university and his Christianity (his wife is also an Episcopal priest) in his book *Meeting Jesus Again for the First Time* (San Francisco: HarperSanFrancisco, 1994). That book, much used in churches, explores potential meanings of his historical Jesus scholarship for Christian life (vii): "Jesus was a spirit person, a subversive sage, social prophet, and movement founder who invited his followers and hearers into a transforming relationship with the same Spirit that he himself knew, and into a community whose social vision was shaped by the core value of compassion" (119).

30. See, for example, Dale C. Allison, *Jesus of Nazareth* (Minneapolis: Augsburg Fortress, 1998), 116–17.

31. Richard B. Hays, "The Corrected Jesus," *First Things* 43 (1994): 43–48.

32. Johnson discovers that Jesus: (1) was a human person; (2) was a Jew; (3) was of the tribe of Judah; (4) was a descendant of David; (5) had a mission to the Jews; (6) was a teacher; (7) was tested; (8) prayed using the word *Abba;* (9) prayed for deliverance from death; (10) suffered; (11) interpreted his last meal with reference to his death; (12) underwent a trial; (13) appeared before Pontius Pilate; (14) antagonized some Jews enough to be involved in his death; (15) was crucified; (16) was buried; (17) appeared to witnesses after his death.

33. Johnson uses Socrates as an analogy: We really do not have the "historical Socrates"; we have the Socrates of Aristophanes, the Socrates of Xenophon, and the Socrates of Plato. The historical Socrates cannot be distinguished from "the Socrates of his interpreters" (106). Yet Johnson's solution of reverting to the narrative frameworks of the four canonical gospels and Acts surely is venturing too far into historical agnosticism, even if they are "all we really have" (102).

34. Hal Taussig, "Jesus in the Company of Sages," in *Profiles of Jesus,* 193.

35. Miller, *The Jesus Seminar,* 79–92.

36. As William Reiser noted, "The fact that so little can be known with certainty about the historical figure Jesus of Nazareth does not give us theological permission to rest the major part of our christological case on the *literary character* of Jesus conveyed to us by the evangelists, or to turn our reflective attention too quickly to the variety of modes of Christ's real presence to the church." See William Reiser, "The Eclipsing of History? Luke Timothy Johnson's *The Real Jesus,*" *Horizons* 24:1 (1997): 122–23. Reiser's view is echoed by N. T. Wright who said that Johnson was "putting the clocks back to the 1890's, when the Germans said that all this historical Jesus nonsense shows that we shouldn't be trying to find the Jesus behind the Gospels at all." See *Time* (April 8, 1996): 58.

37. Ben Witherington III, *The Jesus Quest* (Downers Grove, IL: InterVarsity Press, 1997), 42–57. His view of the group is symbolized by the title of this chapter: "Jesus the Talking Head."

38. Miller, *The Jesus Seminar,* 110.

39. Ibid.

40. N. T. Wright, "Five Gospels but No Gospel: Jesus and the Seminar," in *Authenticating the Activities of Jesus* (ed. Bruce Chilton and Craig A. Evans; Leiden: Brill, 1999), 83–120. See also N. T. Wright, *Jesus and the Victory of God* (Minneapolis: Fortress, 1996), 30.

41. N. T. Wright, *Who Was Jesus?* (Grand Rapids: Eerdmans, 1992), ix.

42. N. T. Wright, *The New Testament and the People of God* (Minneapolis: Fortress, 1992). The third volume of this "Christian Origins and the Question of God" series is N. T. Wright, *The Resurrection of the Son of God* (Minneapolis: Fortress, 2003).

43. See, for example, *Jesus and the Victory of God,* 9–10, 16, 94, 104, 137, 186, 197, 263. Wright's critical realism was inspired by Ben F. Meyer. See, for example, Meyer's *Critical Realism and the New Testament* (Princeton Theological Monographs 17; Allison Park: Pickwick, 1989).

44. N. T. Wright, "In Grateful Dialogue," in *Jesus and the Restoration of Israel* (ed. Carey Newman; Downers Grove, IL: InterVarsity, 1999), 254, 259. Wright is noted for using the lower-case *g* for *god*.

45. In part, Wright owes this insight to his Oxford University mentor, George B. Caird (with whom Marcus Borg also studied).

46. Wright, *The Resurrection of the Son of God,* 718.

47. Noted by Edgar V. McKnight, *Jesus Christ in History and Scripture* (Macon, GA: Mercer University Press, 1999), 240.

48. Wright, "In Grateful Dialogue," 246.

49. See James D. G. Dunn, *Jesus Remembered* (Grand Rapids: Eerdmans, 2003), 472–77, who calls it Wright's *idée fixe*.

50. Mark Allan Powell, *Jesus as a Figure in History* (Louisville: Westminster/John Knox, 1998), 65–81.

51. A phrase and point of view expressed by Vernon K. Robbins, cited by Gustav Niebuhr, "The Jesus Seminar Courts Notoriety," *Christian Century* (November 23, 1988): 1061.

52. As noted in later chapters, it is much more likely that Jesus shared the eschatological *expectations* of his mentor John the Baptist and the early Christian church that was established in his name.

53. Some members of the Seminar, such as Stephen Patterson, depend upon the stratification of Q for their reconstruction of a noneschatological Jesus. Others, such as Marcus Borg, however, do not rely on (or accept) the stratification of Q. Noted by John Kloppenborg, "Discursive Practices in the Sayings Gospel Q and the Quest of the Historical Jesus," in *The Sayings Source Q and the Historical Jesus* (ed. A. Lindemann; Leuven: Leuven University Press, 2001), 161.

54. See Vernon K. Robbins, "Pragmatic Relations as a Criterion for Authentic Sayings," *Forum* 1:3 (1985): 35–63.

55. Miller, *The Jesus Seminar*, 75.

Chapter Four: The Eschatological Prophet and the Restoration of Israel

1. E. P. Sanders, *The Historical Figure of Jesus* (London: Penguin, 1993), 8.

2. E. P. Sanders, *Paul and Palestinian Judaism* (Philadelphia: Fortress, 1977).

3. See also, E. P. Sanders, *Jesus and Judaism* (Philadelphia: Fortress, 1985), 336.

4. Sanders uses the term *eschatology* "to refer to the expectation of an imminent end to the current order" (376).

5. He also adds, in a sentence that caught my eye the first time I read this book in 1986, that this reconstruction may make modern

people look at Jesus askance, but that Jesus was a "reasonable" first-century visionary, not a "weird" one (333).

6. Most clearly stated in John Dominic Crossan, *Jesus: A Revolutionary Biography* (San Francisco: HarperCollins, 1994), 108–12.

7. This difference between a "thin" description and a "thick" one is noted by John K. Riches, *A Century of New Testament Study* (Valley Forge: Trinity Press, 1993), 117. Riches declares that there are "manifold problems" with the idea that the action symbolized the restoration of the temple: "Certainly there is nothing compelling in the evidence to suggest that Jesus looked for its restoration" (118–19).

8. Dale C. Allison, Jr., *Jesus of Nazareth: Millenarian Prophet* (Minneapolis: Fortress, 1998), 98.

9. This is another point made by Allison (*Jesus,* 101) in his powerful rebuttal of objections to Sanders's position raised by Marcus Borg, *Jesus in Contemporary Scholarship* (Harrisburg, PA: Trinity Press International, 1994), 74–90.

10. John P. Meier, *A Marginal Jew: Rethinking the Historical Jesus* (Vol. II; New York: Doubleday, 1991), 465.

11. Borg, *Jesus in Contemporary Scholarship,* 82.

12. Amos Wilder, *The Language of the Gospel: Early Christian Rhetoric* (rev. ed.; New York: Harper & Row, 1971). See also the arguments by Gerd Theissen and Annette Merz in *The Historical Jesus* (Minneapolis: Fortress, 1996), 348, 381.

13. John S. Kloppenborg (Verbin), *Excavating Q* (Minneapolis: Fortress, 2000), 385–86.

14. Allison, *Jesus,* 114.

15. Noted by Allison (*Jesus,* 84–85) who in turn cites Yonina Talmon, "Pursuit of the Millennium: The Relation between Religious and Social Change," *Archives européennes de sociologie* 3 (1962): 130.

16. For example, Jesus' demand for *vertical generalized reciprocity,* a redistribution from the advantaged to the disadvantaged that expects nothing in return (e.g., Luke 14:13–14).

17. Borg, *Jesus in Contemporary Scholarship,* 21.

18. Ben Witherington's argument against Sanders—that Jesus spoke only of the "possible imminence" of the end—is most assuredly wishful thinking, and, it seems to me, is an example of what Sanders opposes: theology controlling exegesis. For example, Witherington's identification of the kingdom coming with power—with some people

not "tasting death" (Mark 9:1)—with the transfiguration six days later (in Mark) is indefensible. See Ben Witherington III, *Jesus the Seer* (Peabody, MA: Hendrickson, 1999), 264.

19. Dale C. Allison, Jr., "Jesus and the Covenant: A Response to E. P. Sanders," *Journal for the Study of the New Testament* 29 (1987): 57–78.

20. Published as Dale C. Allison, Jr., *The End of the Ages Has Come* (Philadelphia: Fortress, 1985).

21. Dale C. Allison, Jr., "A Plea for Thoroughgoing Eschatology," *Journal of Biblical Literature* 113/4 (1994): 651–68.

22. He writes, in conclusion: "I myself do not know what to make of the eschatological Jesus. I am, for theological reasons, unedified by the thought that, in a matter so seemingly crucial, a lie has been walking around for two thousand years while the truth has only recently put on its shoes. But there it is" (668).

Allison returns to this topic in his two most recent works. In *The Apocalyptic Jesus: A Debate,* he offers three ways in which Jesus as an apocalyptic prophet can be relevant for "contemporary faith": (1) Since most of "popular Christianity" is a form of Docetism that in practice denies Jesus' true humanity, the fact that Jesus made a mistake in such a central aspect of his teaching glaringly and helpfully illustrates his true humanity. (2) Jesus' eschatology is "an imperative." Jesus looks backward as well as forward and engrosses himself in how the will of God should be lived in that kingdom: "He lived against injustice because he dreamed of its opposite" (150). (3) Eschatology "can be only parables of faith." Jesus believes in the righteous and compassionate God who demands justice. See Dale C. Allison, Marcus J. Borg, John Dominic Crossan, and Stephen J. Patterson, *The Apocalyptic Jesus: A Debate* (ed. Robert J. Miller; Santa Rosa: CA: Polebridge, 2001), 147–52.

In *Resurrecting Jesus,* Allison likewise claims, "an errant Jesus was a rather effective antidote to a piety that denies Jesus' humanity" (147). He also interprets Jesus' eschatology as mythology that directs us beyond this world. What "premoderns" took literally, he "must take figuratively." See Dale C. Allison, *Resurrecting Jesus* (New York: T & T Clark, 2005), 147.

23. Allison's list of "family characteristics" that locate Jesus' program within the millenarian movement category includes: (1) Addressing the disaffected during a period of social change that threatened traditional symbolic universes and emerging in a time of national

aspirations for independence; (2) seeing the present and near future as times of suffering and/or catastrophe; (3) envisioning a holistic "righting of wrongs" with a promised redemption through a reversal of current circumstances; (4) depicting the reversal as imminent; (5) being both revivalistic and evangelistic; (6) perhaps promoting egalitarianism; (7) dividing the world dualistically into two camps, the saved and the unsaved; (8) breaking hallowed customary religious taboos; (9) being both nativistic and focusing on the salvation of the community; (10) replacing traditional familial and social bonds with fictive kin; (11) mediating the sacred through new channels; (12) demanding intense commitment and unconditional loyalty; (13) focusing on a charismatic leader; (14) understanding its beliefs to be a product of special revelation; (15) taking a passive political stance in expectation of a divinely-wrought deliverance; (16) expecting a restored paradise that would return the ancestors; (17) insisting on the possibility of experiencing utopia as a present reality; (18) growing out of a precursor movement; (19) surviving by coming to terms with disappointed expectations when the mythic end does not arrive (61–64, 78–94).

24. C. J. Cadoux, *The Historic Mission of Jesus* (London: Lutterworth, 1941), 192.

25. Robert W. Funk, *Honest to Jesus* (New York: HarperCollins, 1996), 205.

26. Paula Fredriksen, *Jesus of Nazareth: King of the Jews* (New York: Knopf, 1999).

27. Noted in Steven M. Bryan, review of Paula Fredriksen, *Jesus of Nazareth, Journal of Theological Studies* ns 53:1 (2002): 184.

28. John S. Kloppenborg, "As One Unknown, Without a Name? Co-opting the Apocalyptic Jesus," in *Apocalypticism, Anti-Semitism, and the Historical Jesus* (ed. John S. Kloppenborg and John W. Marshall; London: T & T Clark International), 22–23.

29. Bruce J. Malina, "Christ and Time: Swiss or Mediterranean?" in *The Social World of Jesus and the Gospels* (London: Routledge, 1996), 185, 210.

Chapter Five: The Mediterranean Jewish Peasant and the Brokerless Kingdom

1. John Dominic Crossan, *A Long Way from Tipperary* (San Francisco: HarperSanFrancisco, 2000), 204.

2. Even so, Crossan is driven to discuss historicity for five reasons: (1) Once the issue of historicity was raised during the Enlightenment, it could not be ignored. But the Enlightenment, Crossan argues, was also the "Endarkenment," because these ancient stories were told metaphorically by ancient peoples, but we were "dumb enough" to take them literally. (2) History does matter, especially history reconstructed beyond a reasonable doubt. (3) It is an ethical imperative not to claim "our" story is fact and true and "theirs" is myth and lie, if both stories (e.g., Jesus and Buddha) are powerful and particular parables. (4) Christians believe that Jesus is the incarnation of Yahweh, the Jewish God. That incarnation took place at a particular place and time; it is, in other words, about history, both there and then and here and now. (5) The deep fissure between body and soul, flesh and spirit, in Western sensibility goes against the striving of earliest Christianity to retain its Jewish roots of being enfleshed spirits or spiritual flesh (147–50).

3. John Dominic Crossan, *In Parables: The Challenge of the Historical Jesus* (New York: Harper & Row, 1973), xiii.

4. See David B. Gowler, *What Are They Saying About the Parables?* (Mahwah, NJ: Paulist, 2000), 28–32.

5. Crossan, *A Long Way from Tipperary,* 125.

6. Vernon K. Robbins, "Picking Up the Fragments: From Crossan's Analysis to Rhetorical Analysis," *Foundation and Facets Forum* 1:2 (1985): 31–64.

7. Ibid. As Crossan later notes in his autobiography, he did not start focusing on the life of Jesus as a whole, on words and deeds, until the late 1990's (177).

8. John Dominic Crossan, *Four Other Gospels: Shadows on the Contours of Canon* (Minneapolis: Winston, 1985).

9. Three of the four extracanonical texts Crossan examines will end up in his *The Historical Jesus* as being from the earliest stratum (30–60 CE) in his chronological stratification — the Gospel of Thomas, Egerton Papyrus 2, and the "Cross Gospel" (see below) in the Gospel of Peter. Crossan places the fourth text, the Secret Gospel of Mark, in the

second stratum (60–80 CE). He finds these four extracanonical gospels to be the most important ones to place "in dialectic" with the four canonical gospels (10).

10. Another controversial conclusion is found in chapters 6 and 7, where Crossan—with some caveats—accepts Morton Smith's "reported discovery" at the Greek Orthodox monastery of Mar Saba (approximately halfway between Bethlehem and the Dead Sea) of a letter from Clement of Alexandria that refers to the Secret Gospel of Mark. Crossan argues that the story of the "resurrected youth" in the Secret Gospel of Mark is an independent development of the story of the raising of Lazarus in John 11 from a "common source" (119). Although Clement of Alexandria argued that the Gospel of Mark was written first and the Secret Gospel of Mark was produced later, Crossan reverses the order, arguing that the canonical Mark is "a very deliberate revision of *Secret Mark*" (107–8). He then postulates, in "one of the most complicated cases imaginable," that the canonical Mark "carefully dismembered" that story and "distributed the textual debris at various locations in the gospel" (120). For the view that Smith's discovery was a hoax, see Stephen Carlson, *The Gospel Hoax: Morton Smith's Invention of Secret Mark* (Waco: Baylor University Press, 2005).

11. John Dominic Crossan, *The Cross That Spoke: The Origins of the Passion Narratives* (San Francisco: Harper & Row, 1988).

12. The majority view that the Gospel of Peter was dependent upon the canonical gospels was established by J. Armitage Robinson in 1892 at Cambridge University just three days after the text appeared in Cambridge. Crossan implies that this position reinforces (or is caused by) theological concerns. As Robinson stated: "And so the facts are just what they should be, if the Church's universal tradition as to the supreme and unique position of the Four Canonical Gospels is still to be sustained by historical criticism" (ix). This theological concern is echoed—albeit more delicately—by many modern scholars. Joel B. Green's review of *The Cross That Spoke* (*Journal of Biblical Literature* 109 [1990]: 358), for example, found Crossan's willingness to use "late" noncanonical texts as more reliable testimony than "earlier" canonical texts "troublesome." Is the problem the chronology—that Crossan addresses—or the canonicity?

13. Crossan's primary response is that the story of the two heavenly beings in the Gospel of Peter 9:36–10:40 is followed by both Luke

(24:4) and John (20:12), but not Matthew (28:2–5). Crossan further adds that Matthew, Luke, and John consider Mark to be their "primary and dominant source" and elect to add to Mark with sections of the Cross Gospel but not to replace Mark (19).

14. R. H. Fuller, review of John Dominic Crossan, *The Cross That Spoke, Interpretation* 45 (1991): 71. Note, however, that John P. Meier argues the opposite for Mark 10:46–52: the naming of Bartimaeus is evidence for the tradition's antiquity (see chapter 6 below).

15. Noted by Helmut Koester, *Ancient Christian Gospels* (Philadelphia: Trinity Press International, 1990), 219.

16. John Dominic Crossan, *The Historical Jesus: The Life of a Mediterranean Jewish Peasant* (San Francisco: HarperSanFrancisco, 1991).

17. As Kloppenborg notes, Crossan is not dependent upon this stratification for his conclusion; both Q^1 and Q^2 are in Crossan's oldest stratum (30–60 CE). See John Kloppenborg, "Discursive Practices in the Sayings Gospel Q and the Quest of the Historical Jesus," in *The Sayings Source Q and the Historical Jesus* (ed. A. Lindemann; Leuven: Leuven University Press, 2001), 160.

18. Amazingly, Crossan never refers to Sanders's reconstruction. He refers to Sanders only once; the prologue notes that Sanders believes Jesus was "an eschatological prophet" (xxviii).

19. One example is that of obedient children trusting in a heavenly father who produces the domestic values of generosity, hospitality, familial loyalty, and support. See John H. Elliott, "Jesus Was Not an Egalitarian," *Biblical Theology Bulletin* 32/2 (2002): 85–88; and his "The Jesus Movement Was Not Egalitarian but Family-Oriented," *Biblical Interpretation* 11:2 (2003): 173–210. See also, Diane Jacobs-Malina, *Beyond Patriarchy: The Images of Family in Jesus* (New York: Paulist, 1993).

20. Elliott, "The Jesus Movement Was Not Egalitarian," 206. In a later book, *The Birth of Christianity,* Crossan gives additional evidence that "egalitarianism" existed in antiquity. His examples from Aristophanes and the Mishnah, however, are not overly convincing. More damaging to Crossan's case is that the context of his New Testament example, Acts 2:44–45, actually provides evidence that the early Christian community in Jerusalem was hierarchical, with the apostles as leaders. See John Dominic Crossan, *The Birth of Christianity: Discovering What Happened in the*

Years Immediately After the Execution of Jesus (San Francisco: HarperSan-Francisco, 1998), 470.

21. John Dominic Crossan, *Jesus: A Revolutionary Biography* (San Francisco: HarperSanFrancisco, 1994). An even briefer summary of Crossan's thoughts about the historical Jesus, one written in an easy-to-read question and answer format, can be found in John Dominic Crossan and Richard G. Watts, *Who Is Jesus?* (Louisville: Westminster/John Knox Press, 1996).

22. Crossan, *Tipperary,* 175. The larger book became known as "Big Jesus" between Crossan and his publisher, and this reorganized, popularized, and updated shorter version was known privately as "Baby Jesus": John Dominic Crossan, "Almost the Whole Truth," *The Fourth R* 6:5 (September/October 1993): 7.

23. Crossan later accepted the critique of Amy-Jill Levine that Jesus actually did observe purity codes customary for Jewish peasants of his time and place. See *The Birth of Christianity,* 580–81.

24. James Halstead, "The Orthodox Unorthodoxy of John Dominic Crossan: An Interview," *Cross Currents* 45:4 (1995/96): 510–30.

25. John Dominic Crossan, *Who Killed Jesus? Exposing the Roots of Anti-Semitism in the Gospel Story of the Death of Jesus* (San Francisco: HarperSanFrancisco, 1995).

26. Raymond E. Brown, *The Death of the Messiah* (New York: Doubleday, 1994).

27. Even the "darkness at noon" and Amos 8:9–10, for example, were used by Tertullian to signify a prophecy against Jews (33).

28. Crossan offered another theological defense of the need for historical reconstructions of Jesus in John Dominic Crossan, Luke Timothy Johnson, and Werner H. Kelber, *The Jesus Controversy* (Harrisburg, PA: Trinity Press International, 1999), 1–47.

29. Crossan speaks of the "interface" between oral and scribal cultures (88), but what is missing from his analysis is the recognition that the gospels were created in a *rhetorical* culture, not an *oral* culture. The gospels, for example, give decisive evidence that they were written using the basic exercises in ancient rhetorical handbooks, such as the techniques for expanding or condensing *chreiai*. See Vernon K. Robbins, "Writing as a Rhetorical Act in Plutarch and the Gospels," in *Persuasive Artistry: Studies in New Testament Rhetoric in Honor of George A.*

Kennedy (ed. Duane F. Watson; Sheffield: JSOT, 1991), 157–86; Vernon
K. Robbins, "The Chreia," in *Greco-Roman Literature and the New Tes-
tament* (ed. David E. Aune; Atlanta: Scholars, 1988), 1–23; and David B.
Gowler, "The Chreia," in *The Historical Jesus* (ed. A. J. Levine, Dale C.
Allison, Jr., and John Dominic Crossan, *Princeton Readings in Religion;*
Princeton: Princeton University Press, 2006), 132–48.

30. The "voice" of the itinerants can be found within the Q document; the voice of the householders can be found within the Didache
(354).

31. See David B. Gowler, "'At His Gate Lay a Poor Man': A Dialogic Reading of Luke 16:19–31," *Perspectives in Religious Studies*
32:3 (2005): 249–65.

32. John Dominic Crossan and Jonathan L. Reed, *Excavating
Jesus: Beneath the Stones, Behind the Texts* (San Francisco: HarperSan-
Francisco, 2001).

33. The top ten archaeological discoveries are: (1) The ossuary of
the high priest Caiaphas, which was discovered in 1990. (2) The inscrip-
tion naming Pontius Pilate, which was found in Caesarea Maritima in
1962. This artifact gave evidence that Pilate was prefect, not the lesser
role of procurator. (3) The ruins at Capernaum that excavators
(1968–85) deemed to be the house of Peter the Apostle. (4) The first-
century boat that was discovered in the Sea of Galilee in 1986. (5) The
remains of Yehochanan, a first-century man who had been crucified.
Found in 1968, these are the only remains of a crucified person that have
been found in Palestine. A nail from his crucifixion was found in his
right anklebone, and his arms had been tied to the cross, not nailed. (6)
The sites of Caesarea Maritima and Jerusalem which have yielded
tremendous artifacts and evidence of the first century, especially the
monumental building projects of Herod the Great. (7) The sites of Sepphoris and Tiberias built by Herod Antipas have shown the Greco-
Roman architectural veneer that Antipas imposed in his urbanization of
Galilee. Sepphoris—just four miles from Jesus' hometown of
Nazareth—has yielded spectacular discoveries, such as a Roman-style
theater, a massive underground aqueduct, and the famous Dionysiac
mosaic. (8) The sites of Masada and Qumran are monuments to Jewish
resistance against Rome in the first century. (9) The sites of Jodefat and
Gamla, two villages that lay undisturbed since their destruction by the
Romans in 67 CE, have been excavated by Israeli archaeologists. Since

no other structures were built on top of them, they give an archaeological snapshot of Jesus' life in the first century. (10) Stone vessels and ritual baths are found wherever Jews lived in Galilee and Judea. Both of these items are connected to ritual purity concerns and signify the determination of first-century Jews to remain a distinct people.

34. Crossan and Reed's top ten exegetical discoveries include: (1) The Dead Sea Scrolls give us direct evidence of the life and thought of the Essenes who lived at Qumran. (2) The Nag Hammadi Codices demonstrate the diversity of Christianity. (3) Matthew and Luke both use Mark as a source, which illustrates the need for "excavation" of these texts. (4) Matthew and Luke both also use the Q Gospel as a source. (5) The Gospel of John uses Mark, Matthew, and Luke as sources. (6) The Gospel of Thomas, found in the Nag Hammadi library, is independent of the canonical gospels. (7) There is a 37-unit Common Sayings Tradition that the Q Gospel and the Gospel of Thomas share. This tradition gives us significant evidence of the workings of oral tradition. (8) The Didache is independent of the gospels. This position is important because a small collection of Jesus' most radical sayings appears at the beginning of the document and is present in the Q Gospel. (9) The Gospel of Peter includes an early, independent source (The Cross Gospel). (10) Since most early Christian documents are papyrus codices and not scrolls, this gives evidence that the copyists are "ordinary scribes" and "workaday writers," not calligraphic experts.

35. Noted by Dale C. Allison, *Jesus of Nazareth* (Minneapolis: Augsburg Fortress, 1998), 17–18.

36. William Arnal, *The Symbolic Jesus* (London: Oakville, 2005), 20–38, as well as his earlier "The Cipher 'Judaism' in Contemporary Historical Jesus Scholarship," in *Apocalypticism, Anti-Semitism, and the Historical Jesus* (ed. John S. Kloppenborg and John W. Marshall; London: T & T Clark International), 26.

37. Crossan, *Birth of Christianity,* 334.

38. Noted by Dale C. Allison, *The Apocalyptic Jesus: A Debate* (ed. Robert J. Miller; Sonoma: Polebridge, 2001), 91, 149. See also Bruce J. Malina, "Christ and Time: Swiss or Mediterranean?" in *The Social World of Jesus and the Gospels* (London: Routledge, 1996), 185, 210. As I noted in the conclusion of chapter 4, Malina argues that some of what we see as "future-oriented" sayings would be interpreted as "present-oriented" by first-century peasants.

Chapter Six: The Elijah-like Eschatological Prophet

1. John P. Meier, *A Marginal Jew: Rethinking the Historical Jesus* (Vol. II; New York: Doubleday, 1991), 454.

2. Peter Steinfels, "Peering Past Faith to Glimpse the Jesus of History," *New York Times,* December 23, 1991.

3. One indication of how Meier's book differs from Crossan's is that it received the Imprimatur from The Most Rev. Patrick J. Sheridan, VG (as did the second volume). The third volume received the Imprimatur from The Most Rev. Robert A. Brucato, VJ.

4. John P. Meier, *A Marginal Jew: Rethinking the Historical Jesus* (Vol. I; New York: Doubleday, 1991).

5. In his discussion of Jesus' family and early life, Meier agrees that it would have been unusual for a religious Jew in the first century CE not to marry, but he believes that Jesus remained celibate for "religious reasons": his sense of having a unique prophetic call to give himself totally to the mission to Israel in the final, critical moment of its history (342). What Meier leaves unreconciled, however, is that he also claims that Jesus spent "many years of an uneventful life" in Nazareth (317) and had an "insufferably ordinary" life while living there (352). If so, Jesus' unique prophetic call would not have come until later and therefore could not have been the reason for him to choose lifelong celibacy earlier in his life. Meier may be correct about Jesus' celibacy, but his arguments are conflicting.

6. Steven Cory, review of John P. Meier, *A Marginal Jew, Journal of Religion* 73 (1993): 402. The "marginal" Jesus is thus in some respects "distanced" from Judaism and made more amenable to Christianity.

7. Meier cautions about an (over)reliance on traditions concerning other first-century (BCE and CE) miracle-workers. The questionable reliability of the *Life of Apollonius* makes it difficult to speak in any detail of the first-century Apollonius of Tyana as a "parallel figure" to Jesus of Nazareth. Unlike Geza Vermes, Marcus Borg, and others, Meier argues that the traditions about Honi the Circle-Drawer and Hanina ben Dosa do not give us enough evidence to construct portraits of "Galilean charismatic miracle-workers" (581–88).

8. See Gerd Theissen, *The Gospels in Context: Social and Political History in the Synoptic Tradition* (Minneapolis: Fortress, 1991), 60–80, and chapter 7 below.

9. James D. G. Dunn labels Meier's work as a "bridge to the latest phase of the quest." Dunn argues that Meier's first two volumes are more closely aligned with the New Quest, but that his third volume puts him "firmly in the 'third quest.'" See James D. G. Dunn, *Jesus Remembered* (Vol. 1; Grand Rapids: Eerdmans, 2003), 84–85.

10. Meier postulates that the different lists of names for the Twelve (Thaddeus in Mark and Matthew; Jude of James in Luke and Acts) do not reflect developments in the tradition; they instead indicate that sometime during the two-year ministry, at least one member left the Twelve and was replaced (131). It would be easier, however, to argue that the differences in the lists stem from varying traditions.

11. Meier intends to conclude his four-book series on the historical Jesus by examining "The Enigmas Jesus Posed and Was":

Jesus' teaching on the law. Did Jesus the Jew affirm and accept all aspects of the Mosaic law?

Jesus' parables. The parables, for Meier, are "enigmas in riddle-speech," and their relation to Jesus is an enigma as well (646).

Jesus' self-designations. Meier believes that Jesus referred to himself in parable-like riddle-speech meant to tease the mind of his audience into active thought. This approach posed uncomfortable questions instead of supplying pat answers.

Jesus' death. The precise reason(s) why Jesus was executed by a Roman prefect on the charge of claiming to be King of the Jews is "the starkest, most disturbing, and most central of all the enigmas Jesus posed and was" (646).

12. Steve Bryan, review of John P. Meier, *A Marginal Jew, Vol. III, Journal of Theological Studies* ns 53:2 (2002): 623.

13. See Vernon K. Robbins, "Mark 1:14–20: An Interpretation at the Intersection of Jewish and Greco-Roman Traditions," in *New Boundaries in Old Territory* (edited and introduced by David B. Gowler; New York: Peter Lang, 1994), 137–54.

Chapter Seven: The Eschatological Prophet of Social Change

1. Gerd Theissen and Annette Merz, *The Historical Jesus: A Comprehensive Guide* (trans. John Bowden; Minneapolis: Fortress, 1998), 372. The first sentence of this quote is interposed from two paragraphs after the other parts of the quote.

2. See David B. Gowler, "Heteroglossic Trends in Biblical Studies: Polyphonic Dialogues or Clanging Cymbals?" *Review and Expositor* 97:4 (2000): 443–66.

3. Theissen proposed this "ethical radicalism" thesis in a November 25, 1972, lecture at the University of Bonn. The idea was first published in Gerd Theissen, "Wanderradikalismus: literatursoziologische Aspekte der Überlieferung von Worten Jesu im Urchristentum," *Zeitschrift für Theologie und Kirche* 70:3 (1973): 245–71. It has appeared twice in English, and I am using the version found in Gerd Theissen, "Wandering Radicals: Light Shed by the Sociology of Literature on the Early Transmission of Jesus Sayings," in *Social Reality and the Early Christians* (trans. Margaret Kohl; Edinburgh: T & T Clark, 1993), 33–59.

4. See Gerd Theissen, "'Wir haben alles verlassen' (Mc 10:28)," *Novum Testamentum* 19 (1977):161–96; I am using Gerd Theissen, "'We Have Left Everything...' (Mark 10:28)," in *Social Reality and the Early Christians,* 60–93.

5. Gerd Theissen, *Sociology of Early Palestinian Christianity* (trans. John Bowden; Philadelphia: Fortress, 1978).

6. Theissen takes a functionalist approach and assumes that the two basic needs of society are the preservation of order (integration) and the suppression of conflict. In this way, society seeks to maintain a balance of forces. See Gerd Theissen, *Studien zur Soziologie des Urchristentums* (Tübingen: Mohr, 1979), 57.

7. This omission was noted by Elisabeth Schüssler Fiorenza, *In Memory of Her* (New York: Crossroads, 1983), 147. Luke seems to be responsible for the impression that the wandering charismatics were exclusively male. Luke's Gospel is the only one to include "wife" among those left behind (see Luke 18:29; cf. Mark 10:29). Theissen and Merz's *The Historical Jesus,* though, includes an entire section on "Jesus and the women around him," one which explicitly declares that the itinerant charismatics included both men and women (219–25).

Theissen's recent revision and expansion of *Sociology of Early Palestinian Christianity,* however, sometimes slips back into assuming male disciples, *"...wer Haus und Hof, Frau und Kinder verlossen hatte...."* See Gerd Theissen, *Die Jesusbewegung: Sozialgeschichte einer Revolution der Werte* (Gütersloh: Gütersloher Verlagshaus, 2004), 79.

   8. See also, however, the vigorous critique by Richard A. Horsley, *Sociology and the Jesus Movement* (New York: Crossroad, 1989). Horsley argues that Theissen domesticates the Jesus movement by applying sayings addressed to a broader audience only to "wandering charismatics" (43).

   9. John H. Elliott, "Social-Scientific Criticism of the New Testament: More on Methods and Models," *Semeia* 35 (1986): 10.

   10. Gerd Theissen, *The Shadow of the Galilean: The Quest for the Historical Jesus in Narrative Form* (trans. John Bowden; Philadelphia: Fortress, 1987).

   11. Gerd Theissen, *The Gospels in Context: Social and Political History in the Synoptic Tradition* (Minneapolis: Fortress, 1991). This volume includes significant portions of various articles Theissen published in the mid-1980's.

   12. Theissen first noted this context in *Sociology of Early Palestinian Christianity* (91, 95), and a full treatment is found in his article "Lokal- und Sozialkolorit in der Geschichte von der syrophönikischen Frau (Mk 7, 24–30)," *Zeitschrift für die neutestamentliche Wissenschaft* 75 (1984): 202–25.

   13. Theissen concludes that the decisive elements of the sayings of Jesus were handed down by the disciples. The smaller units of tradition ("apophthegms") were handed down by the disciples as well, and they should be attributed to people who had special roles of preaching and teaching in Christianity's earliest days (112–14). Some of the miracle stories, on the other hand, give evidence of a dialogue with popular tales. The miracle stories quickly moved beyond the circle of Jesus' associates and became "folk traditions." In fact, Theissen argues, some of them probably circulated as popular traditions from the beginning— the ones that do not have a "Christian flavor"—and were later ascribed to Jesus, because he had a reputation as a miracle-worker (112). As Theissen argues in a later work, the gospel authors, as "community leaders," had to create an image of Jesus that was consistent with the convictions and traditions of their communities. So, in one sense, they were

gatherers, bearers of tradition, and "conservative" editors who could not stray too far from the traditional beliefs held by their communities. They could not be satisfied, however, just by repeating those traditions; they also had to rework and develop those traditions to claim legitimacy for their new view and how it corresponded to the tradition. The Gospel of John, since it strayed the most from the tradition, has the most "self-legitimizing" elements. See Gerd Theissen, *Gospel Writing and Church Politics: A Socio-rhetorical Approach* (Hong Kong: Theology Division, Chung Chi College, 2001), 3.

14. Theissen and Merz also strike a via media in their belief that the Gospel of Thomas has preserved traditions that are independent of the canonical gospels (38–39).

15. For the complete arguments, see Gerd Theissen and Dagmar Winter, *The Quest for the Plausible Jesus* (trans. M. Eugene Boring; Louisville: Westminster/John Knox, 2002).

16. Gerd Theissen, *Fortress Introduction to the New Testament* (trans. John Bowden; Minneapolis: Fortress, 2003), 16.

17. Gerd Theissen, *A Theory of Primitive Christianity* (trans. John Bowden; London: SCM, 1999), xiii.

18. For a definition of *covenantal nomism,* see the discussion on E. P. Sanders in chapter 4 above.

19. Cf. Dale Allison's view that Jesus rejected covenantal nomism: Dale C. Allison, Jr., "Jesus and the Covenant: A Response to E. P. Sanders," *Journal for the Study of the New Testament* 29 (1987): 57–78.

20. Meeks called this book a "tour de force" in Wayne A. Meeks, review of Gerd Theissen, *A Theory of Primitive Christianity, Interpretation* 55:1 (2001): 78.

21. Gerd Theissen, "Jesus—Prophet einer millenaristischen Bewegung?" in Gerd Theissen, *Jesus als historische Gestalt* (Göttingen: Vandenhoeck & Ruprecht, 2003), 197–228. An English translation is forthcoming from Fortress Press.

22. William R. Herzog II, *Parables as Subversive Speech: Jesus as Pedagogue of the Oppressed* (Louisville: Westminster/John Knox Press, 1994), 3. Jesus' parable of the Rich Man and Lazarus, for example, portrays representatives of two social classes: the wealthy urban elites who had almost everything and the desperate "expendables" at the bottom of the economic ladder who had almost nothing (53–73). The

wealth of the rich man, Herzog notes, was obtained by a systematic exploitation of the poor—a wealth that could be maintained only by a redistribution of goods from the disadvantaged to the elite in society. Thus, the rich man ends up in Hades, and Lazarus is with Abraham. Jesus' point is clear: During their lifetimes, the rich man could have crossed that social and economic chasm (the "gate" to his mansion) between him and Lazarus, but now it is too late. He refused to act as a benefactor to Lazarus, and now that God has intervened, the "gate" becomes an uncrossable chasm (116).

23. William R. Herzog II, *Jesus, Justice, and the Reign of God: A Ministry of Liberation* (Louisville: Westminster/John Knox Press, 2000).

24. William R. Herzog II, *Prophet and Teacher: An Introduction to the Historical Jesus* (Louisville: Westminster/John Knox, 2005), 1. This book is a more general introduction to Herzog's reconstruction of Jesus.

25. Ibid., 7. Herzog rarely uses the Gospel of John and mentions the Gospel of Thomas only once in this work.

26. As argued by Herzog, *Jesus, Justice, and the Reign of God,* 215–16.

27. Elisabeth Schüssler Fiorenza, *Jesus and the Politics of Interpretation* (New York: Continuum, 2000), 31. John Dominic Crossan also notes the lack of "feminist interest" in recent historical Jesus studies in *Jesus and Faith* (ed. Jeffrey Carlson and Robert A. Ludwig; Maryknoll, NY: Orbis, 1994), 151.

28. Elisabeth Schüssler Fiorenza, *Jesus: Miriam's Child, Sophia's Prophet* (New York: Continuum, 1994), 89–90.

29. See the critique by Kathleen E. Corley, *Women and the Historical Jesus: Feminist Myths of Christian Origins* (Santa Rosa, CA: Polebridge, 2002), 15–20. Schüssler Fiorenza, for example, still maintains that Jesus as the prophet of Sophia sought to abolish the (Jewish?) patriarchal family and rejected Jewish purity.

30. See Carolyn Osiek and Margaret Y. MacDonald with Janet H. Tulloch, *A Woman's Place: House Churches in Earliest Christianity* (Minneapolis: Augsburg Fortress, 2006), 2.

31. Corley, *Women and the Historical Jesus,* 141–43.

32. Grant LeMarquand, "The Historical Jesus and African New Testament Scholarship," in *Whose Historical Jesus?* (ed. William E. Arnal and Michael Desjardins; Waterloo, Ontario: Wilfrid Laurier, 1997), 165. As LeMarquand notes, African biblical scholars explore at least four major issues: (1) mission and colonialism, because they are acutely aware of being "evangelized"; (2) suffering and liberation, in light of the difficulties Africa faces; (3) faith, in which the church is more important than the academy; and (4) the African cultural context, especially since similarities exist between the biblical cultural contexts and African contexts today (166–67).

33. Diane B. Stinton, *Jesus of Africa* (Maryknoll, NY: Orbis, 2004), 103.

34. Ibid., 177–218; Kwame Bediako, *Jesus and the Gospel in Africa* (Maryknoll, NY: Orbis, 2004), 21–22. The image of Jesus in the category of "ancestors" is more controversial, as Stinton notes (142).

35. Stinton, *Jesus of Africa,* 171.

36. Carolyn Osiek, "The Feminist and the Bible: Hermeneutical Alternatives," in *Feminist Theological Reconstruction of Christian Origins* (New York: Crossroads, 1989), 113.

Conclusion

1. See Vernon K. Robbins, "Mark 1:14–20: An Interpretation at the Intersection of Jewish and Greco-Roman Traditions," in *New Boundaries in Old Territory* (edited and introduced by David B. Gowler; New York: Peter Lang, 1994), 137–54.

2. Albert Schweitzer, *The Quest of the Historical Jesus* (trans. Dennis Nineham; Minneapolis: Fortress, 2001), 480.

3. See Diane Jacobs-Malina, *Beyond Patriarchy* (New York: Paulist, 1993), 9.

4. See a similar plea in David B. Gowler, "Text, Culture, and Ideology in Luke 7:1–10: A Dialogic Reading," in *Fabrics of Discourse: Culture, Ideology, and Religion; Essays in Honor of Vernon K. Robbins* (ed. David B. Gowler, L. Gregory Bloomquist, and Duane F. Watson; Harrisburg, PA: Trinity Press International, 2003), 125.

5. Gerd Theissen and Annette Merz, *The Historical Jesus: A Comprehensive Guide* (trans. John Bowden; Minneapolis: Fortress, 1998), 393.

6. Jon Sobrino, *Jesus the Liberator* (Maryknoll, NY: Orbis, 1993), 272–73.

7. Charles W. Hedrick, *When History and Faith Collide: Studying Jesus* (Peabody, MA: Hendrickson, 1999), xiii.

For Further Reading: Other Recent or Notable Studies

Becker, Jürgen. *Jesus of Nazareth*. Berlin: Walter de Gruyter, 1998. Focuses on the kingdom of God as the central element of Jesus' message. Jesus developed the Baptist's message of God's wrath into a message of a gracious God turning toward Israel one last time. Jesus' parables bring the kingdom near, people are admitted to the kingdom through table-fellowship, and Jesus' miracles establish the kingdom. Jesus believed that when this kingdom has completely arrived, history will come to an end.

Chilton, Bruce. *Rabbi Jesus: An Intimate Biography*. New York: Doubleday, 2000. This often speculative biography includes insights of modern scholarship from archaeology, social customs, religious beliefs and practices, political forces, and other elements of the first-century Mediterranean world. Chilton portrays Jesus as a "rabbi" or master of Jewish oral traditions, a teacher of the Kabbalah, and a practitioner of a Galilean form of Judaism that emphasized direct communication with God. A crucial element of Jesus' development is his identity as a mamzer (an "Israelite of suspect paternity") in Nazareth and the resulting ostracism from his community.

Corley, Kathleen E. *Women & the Historical Jesus: Feminist Myths of Christian Origins*. Santa Rosa, CA: Polebridge, 2002. Affirms the role of women in Jesus' own community but challenges the assumption that Jesus himself fought ancient patriarchal limitations on women. Jesus critiqued class and slave/free distinctions, but his critique did not extend to unequal gender distinctions. The presence of women among the disciples instead reflects the greater social freedom for women already happening in the Roman Empire.

Dunn, James D. G. *Jesus Remembered: Christianity in the Making. Volume I.* Grand Rapids: Eerdmans, 2003. The first volume of a proposed three-volume history of the first 120 years of Christianity. The essential shape of the Jesus tradition consists of the pre-Easter impact Jesus made on his first disciples, and oral tradition maintained that essential shape. Jesus looked for the imminent arrival of God's royal rule, which would be characterized by eschatological reversal.

Ehrman, Bart D. *Jesus: Apocalyptic Prophet of the New Millennium.* Oxford: Oxford University Press, 1999. Jesus can be best understood as a first-century apocalyptic prophet. Jesus fully expected that the history of the world was coming to an imminent, screeching halt and that God would intervene in the affairs of this world to overthrow the forces of evil in a cosmic act of judgment. A new kingdom would be created on earth, a just and peaceful kingdom ruled by a benevolent God.

Flusser, David. *Jesus.* Jerusalem: Magnes, 1997. A complete revision of his 1968 book, *Jesus,* in collaboration with R. Steven Notley. Jesus embodies what Flusser calls the moral essence of ancient Judaism. Although not really a Pharisee, he was closest to the Hillel school of Pharisaism, which preached love. Jesus connected his tragic death with his divine sonship and prophetic task, and he eventually embraced the conviction that he would be revealed as the Messiah of Israel.

Freyne, Sean. *Jesus: A Jewish Galilean.* New York: T & T Clark, 2004. Utilizes Gerd Theissen's "contextual plausibility" to reconstruct the historical Jesus as a first-century Jewish Galilean and demonstrate how Jesus was conditioned by his environment. Freyne envisions Jesus within a nonmilitaristic restoration eschatology, but drawing on the nonmilitaristic/triumphalist strand of that movement. Jesus was incensed by Roman and Herodian oppression and the decline in conditions of most Galileans. Jesus thus proclaimed an eschatologically motivated renewal agenda: a total trust in Yahweh as expressed in the Jubilee and Sabbath Year legislation. This message proved too dangerous for the temple establishment and the Romans, and it led to Jesus' death.

Gnilka, Joachim. *Jesus of Nazareth: Message and History.* Peabody, MA: Hendrickson, 1997. Although published in 1997, this book is situated firmly in the "New Quest" approach. The kingdom of God is the center of Jesus' teaching, it is a future eschatological salvation, and it is present and experienced in Jesus' ministry through Jesus' words, healings, and associations with those marginalized by society.

Horsley, Richard A. *Jesus and Empire.* Minneapolis: Fortress, 2003. Argues that Jesus initiated alternative communities of covenant renewal that opposed the Pax Romana through exorcisms and healings. Similar to other prophetic leaders, Jesus proclaimed and enacted the Israelite tradition of God's judgment on oppressive rulers and an egalitarian renewal of the Jewish people. Jesus also proclaimed judgment on the temple, its leadership, and Roman rule.

Horsley, Richard A. *Jesus and the Spiral of Violence: Popular Jewish Resistance in Roman Palestine.* San Francisco: Harper & Row, 1987. Reconstructs the historical Jesus as a social revolutionary who actively opposed violence, especially institutionalized oppressive and repressive violence. Among various forms of Jewish resistance (e.g., rebellion, tax-resistance, mass protests, and apocalypticism), Jesus advocated nonviolent social revolution in anticipation of the political revolution being effected by God.

Horsley, Richard A., with Jonathan Draper. *Whoever Hears You Hears Me: Prophets, Performance, and Tradition in Q.* Harrisburg, PA: Trinity Press International, 1999. Argues that Q and Jesus must be understood in their Jewish matrix, and that they were influenced more by the Jewish prophetic tradition than the wisdom tradition. Q was not embedded in itinerant radicalism but in the Mosaic covenantal tradition of renewing the social order.

Keck, Leander. *Who Is Jesus? History in Perfect Tense*. Columbia, SC: University of South Carolina, 2000. The ancient Greeks used the perfect tense to express the ongoing import of completed action; likewise, Keck discusses the ongoing significance of Jesus of Nazareth. He begins with the "permanent particular" (Jesus the Jew), the "embodied future" (Jesus the teacher), the "fractured prism" (Jesus' death and the living God), and the "authorizing judge" (Jesus in the moral life).

Maccoby, Hyam. *Jesus the Pharisee*. London: SCM, 2003. Argues that Jesus not only supported the Pharisees but was a member of their movement. Jesus believed that one must pay attention to every jot and tittle of the law, because that was the best way to implement the love of neighbor. Like Hillel and other Pharisees, however, Jesus allowed room for reforms based on liberal and rational interpretation of the law.

Mahan, Wayne W. *The Taming of Jesus by Christianity*. Lanham, MD: University Press of America, 2001. Argues that all forms of Christianity, from Paul to the Gospel of John to the Nicene Creed, have domesticated and tamed Jesus and his message of "absolute love" from the Sermon on the Mount. Thus Christianity preserves the Jesus it betrays.

Malina, Bruce J. *The Social Gospel of Jesus: The Kingdom of God in Mediterranean Perspective*. Minneapolis: Fortress Press, 2000. Jesus proclaimed the kingdom of God, a theocracy that is a political institution in which religion and economics are embedded. But Jesus did not proclaim God as king; he proclaimed God as patron/father. Jesus' solution to existing social problems was to endure in the present and look forward to the forthcoming political theocracy where God would be Israel's patron.

McKnight, Scot. *A New Vision for Israel: The Teachings of Jesus in National Context*. Grand Rapids: Eerdmans, 1999. Attempts to understand Jesus in "political" terms. Jesus served as a national prophet on a mission to restore Israel by calling the nation of Israel to repentance in light of a coming act of judgment by God.

Moxnes, Halvor. *Putting Jesus in His Place: A Radical Vision of Household and Kingdom*. Louisville: Westminster/John Knox, 2003. Examines the role of space and place. Jesus leaves the central institution of family to seek the companionship of his disciples. Jesus creates a new place, the kingdom of God, over against the established political kingdom. Moxnes attempts to view Jesus' words and activities in terms of their position and function in place, and he envisions Jesus as leaving male space and as destabilizing places. He concludes that Jesus' vision of "imagined place" in Galilee merges the two spatial structures of household and kingdom into the image of the household of God.

Nelson-Pallmeyer, Jack. *Jesus Against Christianity: Reclaiming the Missing Jesus*. Harrisburg, PA: Trinity Press International, 2001. Christianity's content and practice are radically disconnected from the Jesus of history. This process began with the gospel writers and continues through contemporary scholars who separate the historical figure of Jesus from the Christ of faith worshiped in Christian traditions. Nonviolent images of God guided the historical Jesus, grounded his faith, and informed his actions as he exposed and countered a deadly spiral of violence. He revealed a nonviolent God whose generosity offered abundant life.

Nolan, Albert. *Jesus Before Christianity*. Rev. ed. Maryknoll, NY: Orbis Books, 1992. First published in 1972. A South African liberation theologian reconstructs the historical Jesus before Jesus became the domesticated object of Christian faith. He groups aspects of Jesus the first-century Palestinian Jew in four main categories: catastrophe (e.g., the prophecy of John the Baptist), praxis (e.g., the poor and oppressed, healing, forgiveness), good news about the kingdom (e.g., money, prestige, power, the coming of the kingdom), and confrontation (e.g., politics, religion, the temple action, the temptation of violence).

Robinson, James M. *The Gospel of Jesus: In Search of the Original Good News*. San Francisco: HarperSanFrancisco, 2005. The chronicler of the New Quest and participant in the Jesus Seminar reconstructs the "gospel of Jesus," the "original" good news Jesus taught the first disciples. Jesus' trust in God as a caring father led to a radical lifestyle of deprivation and the experience of God's reign as present in the here and now of daily life. Jesus' self-claim was that God was speaking and acting in what Jesus said and did.

Schüssler Fiorenza, Elisabeth. *Jesus: Miriam's Child, Sophia's Prophet.* New York: Continuum, 1999. The Jesus movement was grounded in the experience of God's all-inclusive love, one that had a dream of liberation for every wo/man in Israel. Jesus stressed the goodness and mercy of God, and the Jesus movement probably understood itself as a prophetic movement of Sophia-Wisdom.

Smith, Morton. *Jesus the Magician.* San Francisco: Harper & Row, 1978. Claims that Jesus as miracle-worker best fits within the category of magician. Jesus' activities as a magician include the vision of the descent of God at his baptism, his "compulsive behavior" (e.g., the spirit driving him into the wilderness), an itinerant ministry of healings and exorcisms, the "magical rite" of the eucharist, and other parallels in Jesus' practice and teachings with those of other magicians.

Sobrino, Jon. *Jesus the Liberator.* Maryknoll, NY: Orbis, 1993. The poor have discovered a new image of Christ as "the Liberator," one who lived and died in service of God's kingdom in history.

Stegemann, Ekkehard W., and Wolfgang Stegemann. *The Jesus Movement: A Social History of Its First Century.* Minneapolis: Fortress, 1999. Not a book about the historical Jesus himself, but an excellent introduction to the early phases of the movement inaugurated by him and the first-century historical, social, and economic contexts.

Stegemann, Wolfgang, Bruce J. Malina, and Gerd Theissen, eds. *The Social Setting of Jesus and the Gospels.* Minneapolis: Augsburg Fortress, 2002. Nineteen essays from the fourth international meeting of the Context Group in Tutzing, Germany, in June 1999. These essays use historically-informed social-scientific models to investigate what can be known about the historical Jesus.

Trocmé, André. *Jesus and the Nonviolent Revolution*. Maryknoll, NY: Orbis, 2004. First published in English in 1973. Trocmé explores the "politics of Jesus," especially the social implications of Jesus' proclamation of the kingdom of God and the biblical Jubilee. He argues the "ongoing relevance" of Jesus' ethic of revolutionary nonviolence.

Vaage, Leif E. *Galilean Upstarts: Jesus' First Followers According to Q*. Valley Forge: Trinity Press International, 1994. A social profile of Jesus' first followers in Galilee as attested by the initial literary stratum of Q. He concludes that these "Galilean upstarts" looked very much like Cynics, claimed to be acting as agents of God's kingdom, wandered from town to town trading their wisdom for hospitality, practiced asceticism, looked back to John the Baptist and Jesus as heroes of their movement, and conducted a form of popular resistance to the official truths and virtues of their day.

van Aarde, Andries. *Fatherless in Galilee: Jesus as a Child of God*. Harrisburg, PA: Trinity Press International, 2001. Argues that Joseph played a minimal role in Jesus' life and that Jesus essentially grew up without a father. Such children were marginalized and excluded from being seen as "children of God." Jesus' experience of marginalization provided the foundation for his compassionate ministry to society's outcasts. Jesus, lacking a father, called upon God to act in this paternal role. He thus destroyed conventional patriarchal values by caring for fatherless children within Palestinian society of his day.

Vermes, Geza. *Jesus the Jew*. Philadelphia: Fortress, 1981. First published in 1973. A classic work that situates Jesus within "charismatic Judaism." Charismatic Judaism, which has an emphasis on miracle working, was more prevalent in Galilee than in Judea. Jesus resembles Hasidim like Honi the Circle-Drawer and Hanina ben Dosa, although Jesus and his teaching have "incomparable superiority." Jesus avoided the term *Messiah,* preferred the term *prophet,* and probably saw himself in the miracle-working tradition of Elijah and Elisha.

Wink, Walter. *The Human Being: Jesus and the Enigma of the Son of Man*. Minneapolis: Augsburg Fortress, 2002. Explores the hypothesis that "the son of the man" figure is a catalyst for human transformation. Wink attempts to construct a "Christology from below" by using the son-of-the-man sayings as his guide. He concludes that the "myth of the human Jesus" is what Christianity needs: A bearer of the archetype of the Human Being, Jesus activates the numinous power that is capable of healing, transforming, or rebirthing those who surrender to it.

Other Books in This Series

Other Books in This Series